WING CHUN
WISDOM

José M. Fraguas

EMPIRE BOOKS/AWP LLC
Los Angeles, CA

DISCLAIMER: Please note that the author and publisher of this book are **NOT RESPONSIBLE** in any manner whatsoever for any injury that may result from practicing the techniques and/or following the instructions given within. Since the physical activities described herein may be too strenuous in nature for some readers to engage in safely, it is essential that a physician be consulted prior to training.

First Edition published in 2024 by AWP LLC/Empire Books.

First Edition Copyright © 2024 AWP LLC/Empire Books. All rights reserved. No part of this publication may be reproduced or utilized in any form or by any means, electronic or mechanical, including photocopying, recording, or by any information storage and retrieval system, without prior written permission from AWP LLC/Empire Books.

EMPIRE BOOKS
P.O. Box 491788
Los Angeles, CA 90049

First edition. Library of Congress Catalog Number:
ISBN-13: **978-1-949753-67-7**

24 23 22 21 20 19 18 17 16 15 14 13 12

Library of Congress Cataloging-in-Publication Data:

Wing Chun Wisdom, by José M. Fraguas — ed. p. cm.
ISBN 978-1-949753-67-7 (pbk.: alk. paper) 1. Martial arts—philosophy
I. Title. GV1114.3.F715 20711161.815'3—dc22

2006019453

PRINTED IN THE UNITED STATES OF AMERICA

TABLE OF CONTENTS

Dedication — *i*

Acknowledgments — *iii*

About the Author — *v*

Foreword — *vii*

Introduction — *xiii*

History — 1

Philosophy — 71

Technique — 173

"Strategy without tactics is the slowest route to victory.

Tactics without strategy is the noise before defeat."

—**Sun Tzu**

DEDICATION

This book is dedicated to my parents, who brought me into this world, gave me love and support, and helped me to believe that I had the power to pursue my dreams.

To the memory of Wong K. Yuen, who taught me my first kung-fu kuen and helped me to understand Chinese culture as way of life, work, and art.

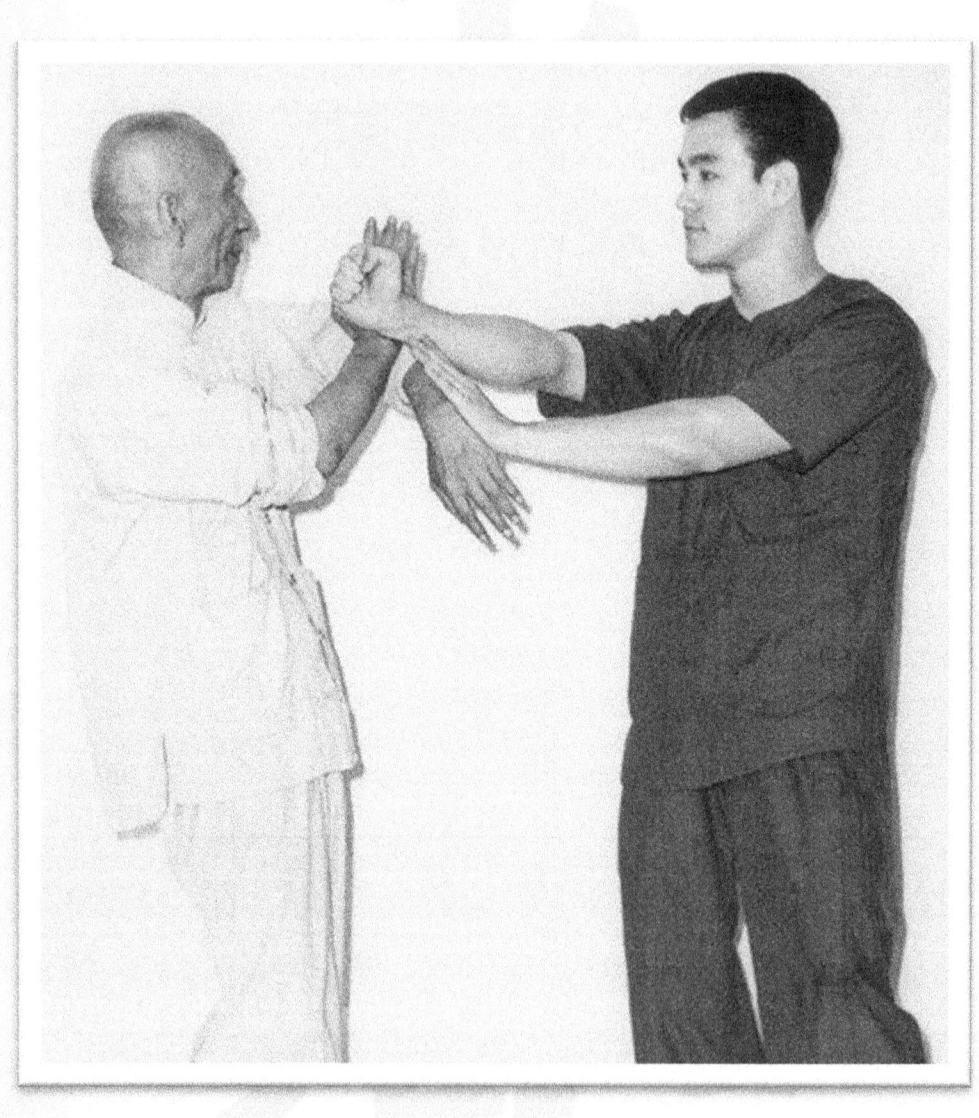

ACKNOWLEDGEMENTS

I would like to thank all the instructors appearing in this book for supplying me not only with enormous amounts of their personal time for the long interviews, but also with wonderful pictures from their personal archives to illustrate this work.

Special thanks to Sifu Tony Massengill—a direct student of the Ip Man's Family system—for allowing me to use the excellent "History" chapter he wrote for his book, *Mastering Wing Chun: The Keys to Ip Man's Kung Fu* (Empire Books). Your friendship and dedication to the art of Wing Chun is greatly appreciated.

José M. Fraguas

詠春功夫

ABOUT THE AUTHOR

Born and raised in Madrid, Spain, Jose "Chema" Fraguas began his martial arts studies with judo, in grade school, at age 9. From there he moved to taekwondo and then to kenpo karate, earning a black belt in both styles. During this same period, he also studied shito-ryu karate and eventually received a seventh-degree black belt.

He began his career as a writer at age 16 by serving as a regular contributor to martial arts magazines in Great Britain, France, Spain, Italy, Germany, Portugal, Holland, and Australia. Having a black belt in three different styles allows him to better reflect the physical side of the martial arts in his writing. "Feeling before writing," Fraguas says.

In 1980, he moved to Los Angeles and was accepted as a student by Dan Inosanto at the Kali Academy. In his first struggling years he managed to meet numerous martial arts greats such as Gene LeBell, Hawkins Cheung, Jun Chong, Wally Jay, et cetera. He trained at the legendary Main Street

Boxing Gym in downtown L.A. in order to learn the "boxing hands" recommended by Dan Inosanto. The open-minded mentality taught at the Kali Academy helped him to develop an eclectic approach to the martial arts. Seeking to supplement and expand his personal training, he researched other disciplines such as wing chun, savate, muay Thai, wrestling, and jiu-jitsu.

In 1986, Fraguas founded his own book and magazine company in Europe, authoring dozens of books and distributing his magazines to 35 countries in three different languages. His reputation and credibility as a martial artist and publisher became well known to the top masters around the world.

Considering himself a martial artist first and a writer and publisher second, Fraguas feels fortunate to have had the opportunity to interview many legendary martial arts teachers. He recognizes that much of the information given in the interviews helped him to discover new dimensions in the martial arts.

"I was constantly absorbing knowledge from the great masters," he recalls. "I only trained with a few of them, but intellectually and spiritually all of them have made very important contributions to my growth as a complete martial artist."

Steeped in tradition yet looking to the future, Fraguas understands and appreciates martial arts history and philosophy and feels this rich heritage is a necessary steppingstone to personal growth and spiritual evolution. His desire to promote both ancient philosophy and modern thinking provided the motivation for writing this book.

"If the motivation is just money, a book cannot be of good quality," Fraguas says. "If the book is written to just make people happy, it cannot be deep. I want to write books so I can learn as well as share."

The author currently lives in Los Angeles.

FOREWORD

As early as I can remember, my house was filled with books. Many of these books—some new, some old—were excellent collections of quotations. My father and mother clipped quotes from magazines or newspapers, and even wrote some themselves and posted them on kitchen cabinets, the refrigerator, and other special places for the family to see.

There are many pleasures to be derived from a book on quotations. There is the relief of finding something that has been buzzing in our minds; there is also the pleasure of finding some thought of which we approve but which we have not managed to express clearly and there is a purely retrospective delight. Of course, wisdom is meaningless until our own experience has given it meaning.

Throughout my childhood, reading and rereading these quotes has helped me to replace negatives thoughts with strong and positive alternatives. While words are not substitutes for the difficult physical and mental training required to master the martial arts, they are a relevant aspect of the transmission and the learning process of every student. *Wing Chun Wisdom* is an anthology of the

best words said by the great teachers of the art. It examines different elements of the art, including its tradition, philosophy, general training, self-defense, et cetera.

All the instructors have expressed similar ideas in very different ways. Regardless of the words they used, there must be truth in the Wing Chun philosophies and principles that so many different people have believed in and lived by. The more I researched, the more I realized that those great teachers are more like you and me than they are different. They had difficult days and seemingly impossible hurdles, yet they endured and prevailed.

I have made every effort to present each quotation within its context as accurately as possible. In philosophical matters, it is syntax—more than vocabulary—that needs to be corrected. Due to the limitations of language and linguistic expression when dealing with philosophical and spiritual matters, it is easy to understand why some of the ideas and principles of these masters are so complex, subtle, and intricate—particularly if the ideas are studied out of context. If you try to apply some of these ideas, don't forget that it is easier to quote somebody else than it is to really understand what they meant by saying it.

There are obvious dangers in using words without being sure what we really mean. But there is another less obvious danger in trying to provide exact definitions—the danger is that we may think we have succeeded. As the philosopher Bertrand Russell wrote: "There is no more reason why a person who uses a word correctly should be able to tell what it means than there is why a planet which is moving correctly should know Kepler's laws." I respectfully would like to advise the reader to *listen* not to the words of the masters, but to *what* they really meant when they said those words. The way of the martial arts produces a practitioner torn between the art and the mystic. The way of the artist and the way of the mystic are similar, but the mystic lacks a craft…the physical techniques.

The craft (physical training) keeps the artist in touch with the remarkableness of the world and in relationship to it. Therefore, philosophy without hard physical training is useless.

This book originated more than 30 years ago as a personal manuscript of life-affirming quotations for my own personal use. As I had the great opportunity to keep interviewing many of the greatest Wing Chun Instructors in the world, the pages of the manuscript kept increasing until one day my mother asked me: "What are you planning to do with all these quotations?" As soon as I answered, "I don't know," she was pointing with her finger to the shelves of one of the bookcases at home where the complete collection of books on quotations was. She simply smiled and left the room.

Meeting the masters and having long conversations with them allowed me to do more than simply scratch the surface of the technical aspects of the art of Wing Chun. It also helped me to research and analyze the human beings behind the teachers.

Years before anyone ever heard of any of them, they devoted themselves to their arts, often in solitude, sometimes to the exclusion of other pursuits most of us take for granted. They worked themselves into extraordinary physical condition and stayed there. They ignored distractions and diversions and brought to their training a great deal of concentration. The best of them got as good as they could possibly get at performing and teaching their chosen art, and the rest of us watched them and, leading our balanced lives, wondered how good we might have gotten at something had we devoted ourselves to whatever we did as ferociously as these masters embraced their arts. In that respect, they bear our dreams.

Most of what passed as human wisdom is merely the post-examination gabble of excited individuals trying to guess how the new lessons will explain the old questions of life and martial arts training. Anything is fresh on the first hearing…even though others may have heard it a thousand times through a score of generations.

In the spring of 2016, I finished the first draft of this work, took the manuscript, and sent it to several Wing Chun teachers. It was exciting to hear their comments. Many of them wrote kind words that they wanted me to use to support the project. Unfortunately, some of them won't see the final printed work because they shed their mortal skin and returned to the sacred battlefields where the true warriors fight their battles. Their words are in this book because without them this work would never be completed.

More than three decades after my mother pointed to that old bookcase, here is the final work. Books are an essential part of my life and they have opened new and exciting avenues of life. My goal is to share these Wing Chun thoughts with as many people as possible. I hope this collection provides comfort and inspiration for all Wing Chun practitioners and martial artists—regardless of style—and for the casual browser and reader. If you, the reader, find this work useful as both a guide and a reference work and discover some unexpected sayings, the book will have served its purpose.

Enjoy.

José M. Fraguas

INTRODUCTION

By
Sifu Tony Massengill

Chinese martial arts are full of exciting stories of the origins of the various systems. Wing Chun is no different. Finding the true history of Wing Chun, or many other Chinese kung fu systems is difficult due to the lack of written records. Stories of the origin have been passed down orally from master to disciple for centuries. Thus, it is possible that names, places, and events are inaccurate.

The stories handed down through the generations hold that the Wing Chun system was developed in the famous Siu Lum (Shaolin) Temple. The system was said to have been taught to a young woman named Yim Wing Chun by a Siu Lum nun named Ng Mui. Yim Wing Chun eventually married a martial artist named Leung Bok Cho, to whom she taught the method. Leung Bok Cho in turn taught Leung Lan Kwai, Leung Yee Tai, Wong Wah Bo, and others. Leung Yee Tai and Wong Wah Bo taught Leung Jan, who became a famous fighter and Chinese doctor. Leung Jan taught his

INTRODUCTION

son Leung Bik, as well as a merchant named Chan Wah Shun. Ip Man (葉問宗師父) was passed the system first by Chan Wah Shun, and then later in Hong Kong by Leung Bik.

There are many books and articles which debate the history listed above. As we have pointed out, with the lack of written records, there is no way of knowing just how accurate this account is. There is also nothing to be gained by arguing over it. So instead of debating the uncertain history of this great system, we will concentrate on what we know to be fact. The Wing Chun system as it has been passed down from the late Grandmaster Ip Man up to the present generation, through the teaching of his sons, Grandmasters Ip Chun (葉準師父) and Ip Ching (葉正師父)

Ip Man was the first to openly teach Wing Chun. He began his teaching career in Foshan, China, and then later in Hong Kong. It is through Ip Man's teaching that Wing Chun has spread throughout the world. Ip Man had many students, but it was Bruce Lee, the famous movie star and "King of Kung Fu" who was the most notable. It was through the fame brought by Bruce Lee that the world became aware of Wing Chun and Lee's teacher, Grandmaster Ip Man.

According to the accounts given to Ip Man's sons Ip Chun and Ip Ching (by Ip Man), their father began his training as a young boy.

Ip Man (1893-1972) was born at Song Yuen of Foshan, China at the end of the Qing Dynasty. Foshan was situated at the most prosperous region of the Guangdong province. Well known masters of the Southern kung fu schools, Wong Fai-hung, Cheung Hung-shing, Leung Jan, Leung Siu-ching, etc., came from Foshan. Ip Man grew up hearing the stories of the exploits of these great kung fu men. So it's not surprising that he would develop into one of the legendary masters himself.

Ip Man's education in Wing Chun began as a youth when he became a student of Chan Wah Shun, who was a student of the famous Leung Jan. Chan Wah Shun rented the Ip family clan hall on the main street of Foshan in order to teach kung fu. He accepted Ip Man as a student towards the end of his teaching career when he was quite old. Master Chan was a big man by Chinese standards, so his kung fu was powerful. Ip Man learned from Master Chan until the masters' death and continued his training with his Sihing (Senior) Ng Chun until Ip Man left Foshan for Hong Kong in 1941.

Ip Man moved to Hong Kong at the age of 15 to attend St. Stephens College. There he had a chance meeting with an old gentleman who was a martial artist. This old man crossed hands with Ip Man and beat him soundly. This disturbed Ip Man very much as he had developed his kung fu to a high level and considered himself to be quite proficient. As it turned out, the old gentleman was Leung Bik, the son of Ip Man's Sifu, Master Chan Wah Shun's teacher, the famous Leung Jan.

INTRODUCTION

Master Leung Bik's Wing Chun was much more refined than what Ip Man had learned from Master Chan. While Chan Wah Shun had been a big man, Leung Bik was much smaller. There was also a pretty wide gap in the education level between the two masters. Chan Wah Shun was not very well educated, while Leung Bik was the son of Leung Jan, who was a well-educated doctor of Chinese medicine. This education was passed to his son. This meant that Leung Bik was better able to understand the underlying principles of the Wing Chun system. This knowledge was passed to Ip Man.

Upon learning all that Leung Bik had to teach him, Ip Man went on to explore ways to simplify Wing Chun, making it easier to understand. In addition to his education in "Wing Chun", Ip Man received an advanced formal education in his youth. He learned the theories and principles of modern science and could therefore make use of modern technological knowledge such as mechanical and mathematical theories to explain the principals of Wing Chun. Ip Man even changed terminology such as "The Five Elements," and "Eight Diagrams" (Ba Gua) which were commonly used in metaphysics. This helped to demystify Wing Chun, thus making it easier for the common student to understand and apply the system.

After completing his Wing Chun education under Leung Bik, Ip Man returned to China. Back in Foshan, Ip Man began teaching a small group of students, including Kwok Fu and Luen Kai. In 1949 Ip Man returned to live in Hong Kong, where he eventually began his public instruction of Wing Chun.

In July 1950, through Lee Man's introduction, Grandmaster Ip Man started teaching in Dai Lam Street, Kowloon. The first Wing Chun Kung Fu class was for the Restaurant

Workers Association. When he opened the class there were only 8 people, including Leung Shang and Lok Yiu. All these were restaurant workers, but later he was joined by Chu Shung Tin, Yip Bo Ching, Chiu Wan, Lee Yan Wing, Law Peng, Man Siu Hung, and others. Grandmaster Ip Man also taught in the Restaurant Workers Shang Wan branch, Union HQ in Hong Kong. Students included Lee Wing, Yue May Keng, Lee Leung Foon, and others.

Over the next 20 years, Ip Man would leave his mark on the world of martial arts by teaching those that would spread Wing Chun across the globe. Some of those who became students of the Grandmaster were Wong Shun Leung, Bruce Lee, and of course Ip Man's sons, Ip Chun and Ip Ching.

The Ip Man Wing Chun system has today become one of the most popular martial art systems in the world. Bruce Lee was initially responsible for bringing Wing Chun to the attention of the world, but it has been through the teaching of today's masters, and most notably Ip Man's sons Ip Chun and Ip Ching that we have full knowledge of the heritage of this great kung fu system.

HISTORY

The Ip Man films have been both a curse and a blessing. They have raised awareness of Wing Chun to new heights, and it is growing exponentially, but it is also spreading so quickly that there is a danger of the quality degrading, particularly as there is no governing body to maintain any quality control.

Shaun Rawcliffe

I was not a "natural" at kung fu because I am not a physically big guy. I do not have strong physical power either. My job was office work. Brain work was used rather than physical power work.

Donald Mak

We are training combat, not paper folding, so there has to be realism involved at all times.

David Peterson

I started this martial art in 1998, at a time when there was no internet or YouTube or anything like that. I couldn't just watch videos to see what exactly you were doing. That's what made it so mystical and mysterious.

Mohammed Ince

Bruce Lee was one of the pioneers who embraced change and growth in the art—combining different styles into his con-cepts and theories that he called Jeet Kune Do.

Carson Lau

Wing Chun is not meant to be a system that produces robots. There is a lot of freedom in the application of Wing Chun, but you have to have the analytical intelligence to see what may not be immediately obvious.

Tony Massengill

Kung Fu is a test of time. In addition to its practicality in self-defense and combat, its true meaning lies in the teachings of discipline and morality to its practitioners, using martial arts to promote benevolence.

Kim Man Chan

I respect my elders and seniors in the system, but I do not necessarily believe that when someone began their study or with whom they studied is the primary criteria for their ranking or status in a system.

Randy Williams

I discovered Wing Chun in 1979 and for the first 10 years I predominately trained in the UK with several Wing Chun instructors. It was May 1989, following a seminar at my school by Sifu Ip Chun that I decided to accept his offer to train with him in Hong Kong.

Shaun Rawcliffe

I agreed to help some of the high school kids in Koo Sang's class with their English, and they in turn invited me into their homes to meet their families.

Alan Lamb

William Cheung and Wong Shun Leung were Bruce's source of information on Wing Chun. They were our seniors, but we couldn't openly let them know what level we were at for fear they wouldn't show us more.

Hawkins Cheung

During my early years, my training was very painful as none of my Kung Fu brother had any mercy, especially one Kung Fu brother who was the most senior. Because of that, I was training even harder.

Lin Xiang Fuk

I believe the future is great for Wing Chun. It has become increasingly popular and more well-known to a greater audience. This is very good as the system spreads and more people want to learn, want to experience and find out the truth of Wing Chun.

Gorden Lu

In old times, we trained almost 365 days a year at least six hours daily. We were totally dedicated and serious about our training and practiced dog hard.

Alan Lee

There are a total of 108 movements in the wing chun wooden dummy form. These movements are considered to be techniques of the higher levels of learning.

Jim Lau

Kung fu also could teach one to handle many difficult situations in life and make solving problems simpler.

Gary Lam

When I began studying martial arts, there were very few legitimate teachers who were practicing openly. It was all a big secret, and when they did consent to teach, they would charge their students an arm and a leg to learn the most basic of techniques.

Alan Lamb

After training for a while with a teacher, I soon realized that if I was going to really accomplish anything in Wing Chun, I would have to seek out Sifu Wong Shun Leung myself. So, toward the end of 1983, that's exactly what I did. The rest is, as they say in the classics... history.

David Peterson

I believe that a true traditional Chinese Kung Fu instructor should teach his students the true morality of martial arts and a sense of knightliness that should be felt in everything he does.

Leung Ting

There are wing chun disciples whose achievements in martial arts are not even second to those of Bruce Lee. But they never made movies and got famous, so no one knows them.

Wong Shun Leung

I am in total agreement with Ip Man's statement that "The distance of fighting or sparring is the distance of Chi Sao." In fighting or sparring, reflex and sensitivity are the major advantage that enables the Wing Chun practitioner to win.

Samuel Kwok

The fact that our Chinese predecessors were able to develop as ingenious a "fighting system" as Wing Tsun does not necessarily mean, as I have often heard, that they also developed a correspondingly ingenious "teaching method".

Keith R. Kernspecht

To see whether the student has this attitude, the good sifu will test him and look for humbleness, desire to learn and perseverance. Those without these characteristics never develop real skill in the system.

Victor Kan

Wing Chun is easy to learn and apply, suits people of all ages and does not require brute strength or acrobatic skills. Its logic and scientific principles appeal to people who are more skeptical nowadays about what they are learning.

Jim Fung

Wing Chun is primarily a striking art and close-range combat is our true strength.

David Peterson

Traditional values always should be there because they represent our roots and education. Practitioners should be responsible not only for their own actions and words but for the future of the arts too. Martial arts are an invaluable tool for use in real life.

Francis Fong

The Wing Chun principles and Chinese code of ethics were created and developed by a long line of traditional teachers, these may differ in the way they are expressed depending on the teacher, but all must have the true philosophy of the Kung Fu art and spirit.

Augustine Fong

Today everyone wants everything NOW. In the old days, a student learned at the pace set by their teacher. Today people are in too much of a hurry and try to rush their training.

Ip Chun

In the old days, we trained five to six days a week; therefore, the sifu was very personal to us. Today, students train two days a week, on average. Everybody rushes in and rushes out. It is hard for sifu and his students to spend time together.

Chung Kwok Chow

One time, Hawkins Cheung and I were discussing fighting techniques, and I threw a punch at him. With one crashing slap, he used "pak da" on me and left an incredible expanding welt on my forearm. I was literally stunned at the power of this small man!

Robert Chu

Students today do not seem to have the patience that was required in the old days. Respect is also a virtue that seems to be lacking in many students in today's world.

Ip Ching

Wing Chun was the gun that Yip Man gave us; the frustrating part was that you had to learn how to aim and shoot. The problem was your target always moved, you couldn't get a fix on it. Wing Chun is a problem solv- ing art.

Hawkins Cheung

Our Wing Chun forefathers designed the form to illustrate specific ideas. Many of these ideas are totally beyond one's imagination if one were simply to see the form played.

Alan Lee

A huge personal benefit was the fact that I was able to communicate with my Sifu in his mother tongue, with little or no need for any translation, thus I didn't miss out on the little details that someone without the language might fail to appreciate.

David Peterson

Bruce Lee left Hong Kong when he was 18 years old and he only knew part of the modified version taught by Yip Man. Perhaps Bruce had to look for answers and solutions outside wing chun because he didn't know enough wing chun and had to fill the gaps.

William Cheung

Confidence and experience go hand-in-hand. If you're not confident, you will be a disaster in driving or fighting. To Confucius, *the centered mind sees clearly*. In life, your yin and yang must be balanced for you to be in the center.

Hawkins Cheung

Although I appreciated the intellectual principles of Wing Chun at an early age, it wasn't until later that I came to appreciate the practicality and effectiveness of Wing Chun in real-life situations.

William Kwok

In China, if the Kung Fu class that teach a student an advance technique at first day, student(s) may feel they are missing some- thing because they know they did not get the good fundamentals yet.

Gorden Lu

Although I enjoy all the martial arts, I have only trained in two systems-wing chun kung-fu and jeet kune do with Sifu Ted Wong.

Randy Williams

My father had to pay off this investigator to have my name wiped from the record, or else I wouldn't have been able to attend college in Australia.

Hawkins Cheung

In the old days, you had to really show respect and learn how to build up a good relationship between your sifu and other senior students before you could learn kung fu. But nowadays, a lot of students just come and learn, then go home.

Au Yeung

I was interested in martial art since I was age 14 (1976), but later, at about 16, I start to look for things that could be more effective in a street fight situation. On those days I was reading the legendary "Real Kung Fu Magazine" the Chief editor was my Si-gung Mr. Leung Ting.

Emin Boztepe

According to my research on other lineages of Wing Chun, such as Red boad Wing Chun or Ban Chung Wing Chun, it was said that the ancient style of Wing Chun has only one form, called *Siu Nian Tau or Siu Nian* which has consisted of all the martial arts elements, such as hand techniques, kicking, stance, stepping etc.

Donald Mak

Wing Chun practitioners must learn to relax, use energy only where necessary, and appropriate and stick to and control the opponent's arms and attacks.

Shaun Rawcliffe

If "Siu Nim Tau" is the ABCs of Wing Chun, and "Cham Kiu" is the grammar and short phrases, what "Chi Sau" does is teach us to "converse" and to make use of this "language" in a very effective and individual way, rather than just being robots who repeat a pattern of sounds.

David Peterson

I believe Ronald Reagan summed it up best, "Peace through superior firepower." In order to really live in peace, one must have the power to wage war effectively.

Tony Massengill

My first instructor inspired all kinds of fear in me. His teaching methods could be brutal at times, with the result of a missed block being a black eye, a lump on the head and/or a fat lip.

Randy Williams

As a teenager, I looked up to my teachers and masters and considered them role models. They embodied the values and discipline of martial arts and were sources of inspiration for me. Their dedication and determination impressed me deeply and I aspired to follow their example. They were not only trainers, but mentors who guided us along the way and helped us develop our skills and character strengths.

Mohammed Ince

HKB Eng Chun is a rare lineage of Wing Chun that has recently come out to the public which has been classified by the VTM (Ving Tsun Museum) as Wing Chun from the secret society era. Currently, there has been great demand and interest in HKB Eng Chun worldwide.

Lin Xiang Fuk

People in old times were looking for less entertainment, more focus on training and training harder.

Gorden Lu

The health aspect is a by-product of hard work that comes from training martial arts. You can go to the gym or do basic exercises with a healthy diet to achieve health benefits.

Carson Lau

Sifu Yip Man once told me to attack him using a long sword against his long pole. When I attacked, I found there was no chance for me to get near him, and he totally defeated me. He then showed me the accuracy and speed of his long pole.

Alan Lee

There is no formal ranking in wing chun kung-fu. Teaching is part of any complete learning process and as a result a few of my more advanced students assist with instruction.

Jim Lau

Watching my Sifu Wong Shun Leung used his Wing Chun against masters of other different arts also gave me long-lasting inspiration for my personal training.

Gary Lam

Not every westerner, nor Chinese or any other genre will take to traditional Chinese training, it is up to us instructors to find and nurture the right ones.

Shaun Rawcliffe

Advances in technology and sports science have also contributed to a greater understanding of biomechanics and human movement, influencing the way techniques are taught and practiced with greater emphasis on efficiency, effectiveness, and injury prevention.

William Kwok

People living in America don't realize how lucky they are. They have such a variety of martial arts knowledge available to them.

Alan Lamb

Wing Tsun is for fighting and real self-defense. A real fight differs from sport tournaments in that there are no rules, no weight divisions, no regulations, etc.

Leung Ting

I firmly believe that wing chun is something very logical. As long as it stays logical it doesn't matter what you call it or what you're actually doing. If it is logical, if it works, use it! Make the art your slave and never allow the art be your master.

Wong Shun Leung

If the system is changed to where it no longer is of the standard Ip Man taught, it shouldn't be called Ip Man Wing Chun. We intend to help correct this by educating the public as to the standard of the Ip Man system as passed to me through the sons of the Grandmaster.

Samuel Kwok

However you spell it, the Wing Tsun (Wing Chun, Ving Tsun) now practiced in most European countries (maybe with the exception of Great Britain) comes from what I taught.

Keith R. Kernspecht

Sifu Yip Man taught me that learning Wing Chun was for self-defense.

Alan Lee

Near the end of 1972, I was told by my kung fu brothers, that Sifu Yip Man was very pale and thin, and he could hardly talk. Yet he was quite pleased to see me rushing back to pay my respects to him. He tried so hard to comfort me, he even tried to put on a little smile.

Victor Kan

If you are serious about learning a genuine Martial Art, you have to find the right master to teach you, regardless of whether he lives in Hong Kong, China, Taiwan or wherever.

Jim Fung

If we stay with "pure," then we're never growing. I think that tradition has value, but I educate students to open their minds to be creative and dynamic, instead of being just a copy.

Francis Fong

In this style, there is no emphasis on weight training because the system does not rely on brute force but on what we call "explosive power."

Augustine Fong

The Confucian text "Doctrine of the Mean" holds a lot of meaning and kinship to Wing Chun. The "Mean" is the middle, or center. Wing Chun is a method based on maintaining the center, and not overreacting one way or the other.

Ip Chun

The founder of the Wing Chun style, since Wing Chun is probably the one and only martial art style invented by a woman. She was probably five feet tall and less than 100 pounds, so with her physical disadvantages, she had to fight smarter, not harder.

Chung Kwok Chow

It is important that we as teachers teach students the value of learning and support them to achieve their goals. We need to show them that learning Wing Tsun is not just a sporting activity, but also a personal journey of growth and self-improvement. Through a combination of challenging training, positive reinforcement, and a motivating environment, we can ensure that students maintain their passion for the martial arts and continue to develop their skills.

Mohammed Ince

My own teacher often had debates with his Sifu, the late Wing Chun patriarch Ip Man, and made changes to the system in order to make it more combat efficient. He did so without abandoning any of the core concepts.

David Peterson

Johnny Wong, a fellow Yip Man wing chun practitioner once said to me that Yip Man told him, "The great secret in wing chun is that it develops your mind and makes you smarter." I think that comment is very telling.

Robert Chu

Kung Fu originally is about being able to protect yourself. This is the chief aim of Wing Chun training.

Ip Ching

Wing Chun is extremely popular and will continue to spread in popularity through word of mouth and through cinema. The Ip Man movies have been a major influence in spreading the popularity of Wing Chun worldwide in the last decade.

William Kwok

Bruce was 100 years ahead of all other martial artists. Read his notes and look at what he was doing. Even today, people don't understand things he said a long time ago. You can see his influence in almost everything related to martial arts and physical fitness. I really think this is his greatest contribution.

William Cheung

Wing Chun's energy is on the legs more than the upper body. Because the Wing Chun hands are used to feel the opponent's hands and read his intentions, the hands must be soft.

Hawkins Cheung

It was known that the pole technique was a gift from exchanging forms with other styles of martial arts in the early days. That came from the time when people were traveling in a boat called "hung shu".

Stephen Chan

We can say that *Ip Man* plus *Gulao* form the complete art of Leung Jan's *Wing Chun system* from both a technical and philosophical point of view. By simplifying the system from three forms to 12 techniques, it is embracing the *Tao Te Ching*'s "art of subtraction".

Donald Mak

I have always been gifted for sport but I did worked very hard on every- thing I got involved into. And why I was training so hard most of my WT classmates really didn't know? It was because I was always the most of the time a target of racial conflict in Germany as a Turkish person. Interestingly enough that racial feeling has not changed even today for a Turkish foreigner with different cultural background in Christian Europe.

Emin Boztepe

Watching my Sifu practicing Chi Sao for the first time, making it all look so easy and effortless.

Shaun Rawcliffe

Recent research suggests that Yuen Kay San may well have been the real force behind the skills and methods of Ip Man, but that because he remained in China, his prowess and expertise was never appreciated outside of the mainland.

David Peterson

As an instructor, I find I am working against YouTube and instructional videos. When I began in Wing Chun in 1979, we were totally reliant on our Sifu. Today, if the Sifu is not teaching the student at a pace that satisfies the student, then the student simply learns the next form or whatever from "Sifu YouTube".

Tony Massengill

Kung-fu is not as easy to learn as many people might think, and not everyone has the intestinal fortitude to put in the hours of sweat required to achieve a high level of skill.

Randy Williams

Styles exist in the Martial Arts because people have an innate desire to express their individuality.

David Peterson

The way I see it, there are changes in the areas of training intensity and consistency. Compare today's Martial Arts, where many people may do it more as a hobby, to the intensity of the past, during revolution and in secret societies.

Lin Xiang Fuk

Ultimately, it depends on individual goals, opportunities and preferences. There are qualified teachers and schools around the world that can provide an excellent education. However, if a deep dive into the origins and culture of martial arts is desired, a trip to Hong Kong, China or Taiwan can be rewarding.

Mohammed Ince

As Ip Man said, "Chi Sao is the heart of Wing Chun." However, no one fights with Chi Sao. True Chi Sao teaches significant fighting techniques, and also trains the students in the elements that we will use in combat.

Gorden Lu

When I learned privately from Sifu Yip Man, he told me he had five other private disciples that he taught basically everything. Because I trained with Yip Man late in his life, he said it was too difficult for him to show me certain things, so he wanted me to find these five disciples and complete my training.

Alan Lee

In spite of learning from the same teacher, practitioners of many different traditional martial arts disagree about what is authentic.

Jim Lau

I consider myself very lucky to train under the legendary Wong Shun Leung. To me, that's more than I could ever ask for. He was the best Wing Chun master/teacher/fighter I have ever seen.

Gary Lam

I met Robert Chu, who is an excellent wing chun teacher. He also spent some time with Koo Sang in Hong Kong. He has a lot of experience and his wing chun technique is very strong.

Alan Lamb

Before I attended my first Wing Chun class, I had practiced judo, karate, and a little bit of Thai kickboxing. But I was a child, and I didn't take any of it very seriously. I have always been a big fan of Bruce Lee's movies which made me want to train his method.

Thommy L. Boehlig

When Grandmaster Yip Man accepted me as his "closed-door student" it was to teach me what we can call a more 'sophisticated' version of the art. He was at an advanced age and many of the applications that he taught and used in his young days were not effective for him anymore because of his age.

Leung Ting

Jeet kune do was simply a personal format Bruce used to apply his knowledge and experiences. I told him most likely there was a missing link in his research and that he was trying to cover too much distance in too short a time.

Wong Shun Leung

Bruce Lee was a great martial artist who learned from Grandmaster Ip Man. He always gave credit to Ip Man and Wing Chun for his accomplishments.

Samuel Kwok

I practiced Wrestling, Judo, Ju-Jitsu, Karate, Aikido, Kempo, Hapkido, Taekwondo, Escrima, Wing Chun, Ving Tsun, Wing Tsun. But none of these styles teaches pure self-defense. Shotokan Karate teaches Shotokan Karate, Ju-Jitsu teaches Ju-Jitsu, Wing Chun teaches Wing Chun.

Keith R. Kernspecht

In the 1970's Bruce Lee did much to boost the Ving Tsun system worldwide. At that time there were not many qualified Ving Tsun teachers around. The system became a victim of its own publicity. Virtually anyone could become a Ving Tsun master overnight.

Victor Kan

Although I have spent more than 50 years training in Wing Chun, I have found that like any other art, there is no limit to my learning development.

Jim Fung

In my opinion, there is no such thing as a pure style. What is pure? That's really old-fashioned. We have to be adaptable because the world is changing. People need to change to adapt with society and cultures.

Francis Fong

Although Wing Chun has its unique techniques and methods, the ultimate goal is the same as some other styles that focus on practical self-defense.

William Kwok

I was one of the first Chinese in teaching Wing Chun in the US. Bruce Lee did it first in Seattle and Oakland before he developed Jeet Kune Do.

Augustine Fong

I began training as a child under my father in Foshan, China. My brother and I began training in Wing Chun at a very early age and continued our training when we joined our father in Hong Kong in 1961.

Ip Chun

When I learned my style of Wing Chun in Hong Kong in the late '60s, my sifu always emphasized the importance of being soft, which took me a long time to achieve.

Chung Kwok Chow

My biggest concern is the growth in politics. Wing Chun should be one large family and it predominantly still is in Hong Kong, but as it grows and spreads there is a risk of any differences breeding an unhealthy competitiveness and criticisms.

Shaun Rawcliffe

In Chinese culture, it is often a custom to exaggerate a friend's credentials when introducing him to another friend. It's a kind of puffery - the only thing is you have to find out whether it is real or not and in what context. It's the same with wing chun or any other martial art.

Robert Chu

Today the student does not have to rely only on his memory, but can easily film the lesson from the teacher, and is able to catch more details of the lesson.

Ip Ching

Bruce at that time was a little bit of immature and I'll dare to say that he had more or less some kind of inferiority complex. This is the reason why he trained so hard. He was constantly practicing and very hungry for wing chun knowledge.

William Cheung

In the mid-1960's Bruce gave a demonstration on a popular talk show on television. Bruce didn't mention anything about Wing Chun but referred to his art simply as "gung-fu." I realized that something must have happened between Bruce and Yip Man.

Hawkins Cheung

Today I understand that I'm lucky to be alive. Wing Tsun was, really, love at first sight and it fit me. For whatever reason, I was a natural at it. I was always looking to prove myself on the streets and I was very aggressive because of the way I lived back then.

Emin Boztepe

To be honest and frank when I started Wing Chun, I had no appreciation of any philosophy or any interest in that side of the martial art. I was a professional bodyguard and wanted a fighting system that would work simply and practically at very close quarters.

Shaun Rawcliffe

The first day I ever met my late Sifu Wong Shun Leung, he said to me, "If you can show me a better way to fight than I am doing now, I want to learn from you!" That is the attitude that you must take if you want to improve both as a person and a practitioner.

David Peterson

Don't get into politics, just train hard and be the best you can be. Judge your kung fu by how practical it is, not on how pretty it looks.

Tony Massengill

The older and more senile I get, the more sense the statement, "I've forgotten more about wing chun than you'll ever learn," makes to me.

Randy Williams

Hek Ki Boen Eng Chun came from the Southern Shaolin, out of the Eng Chun Dim Hall (also known as the Weng Chun Dim) and passed down to the Black Flag Lodge of Hung Men (Secret Society) in Fukien Province.

Lin Xiang Fuk

Naming traditional kung fu schools after a Sifu is also significant in honoring the lineage and traditions of the art. In Chinese culture, there is a great respect for teachers and their lineages, and the Sifu is considered the head of the school, responsible for passing down the martial art to their students.

William Kwok

As a member of Ip Man's family, I feel this is my duty and responsibility to keep the tradition and spread the art and pass it to the next generation and the people who love this art.

Gorden Lu

Over the years, the style has become diluted with many teachers who don't seem to understand the ideas behind Wing Chun, and who don't really understand how to apply it.

Alan Lee

The current non-traditionalist trend was actually fostered by the rigidity of some of the so-called traditionalists.

Jim Lau

The art of Wing Chun remains more or less the same. In the past, (Yip Man's era), Wing Chun wasn't open to non-Chinese, but now it's different.

Gary Lam

The lowest point came when I had to back out of a movie deal. I had written a script for Jim Kelly and myself, and I was able to get funding for the movie, but I was just too ill to follow through.

Alan Lamb

My training under grandmaster Yip Man started when I already knew the basis and fundamentals of the Wing Chun method.

Leung Ting

When Bruce Lee came back to Hong Hong to do movies, we would meet and talk about martial arts for hours. We had a very good relationship until the very end.

Wong Shun Leung

I did exhaustive research, studying with as many of Ip Man's senior level students as I could. I have had the good fortune to have Li Wai Chi, Chan Wai Hong, Chu Sheung Tien, and Wong Shun Leung, among others, share their knowledge with me.

Samuel Kwok

I cannot speak on behalf of all Kung Fu systems or styles, but I can say with a great deal of confidence that Wing Chun in the West has very much "caught up" with the technical level in China/Hong Kong.

David Peterson

"Wu shu" means Martial Art. In the 1980s, the Chinese Government allowed Martial Artists to resume practice but banned the deadly blows of the kung fu system.

Jim Fung

In the mid-50s, Yip Man was not very happy. He had a lot of personal problems. Two of his sons were still inside mainland China and he had a lot of financial burdens. The latter incidents virtually forced him to move his school into a very rough area of Hong Kong called Sab Gik in May 1957.

Victor Kan

I made many mistakes during my training, just like my students do now, but these experiences have made me a more competent teacher and practitioner.

William Kwok

Chi Sao also develops close distance coordination, mobility, balance, timing, accuracy, and the correct use of energy.

Shaun Rawcliffe

In 1981, I met Guro Dan Inosanto. I always liked to try and do different things. I learned from many friends, associates, and different people.

Francis Fong

My Sifu Ho Kam Ming was rich so he had all the time in the world to be with Yip Man, train and to go places with him. He was very fortunate.

Augustine Fong

Wing Chun became one of the most popular kung fu styles in the world because of Bruce Lee, and it still is. Today there are more Wing Chun practitioners than ever before.

Chung Kwok Chow

If a person says that wing chun is over 300 years old, then it is true for all the branches as well, not just one branch, after all, they all are linked through one important period of time—the time of the Red Boat Opera people of the King Fa Hui.

Robert Chu

My father considered Chi Sao to be the genius of the Wing Chun system. I would have to agree with this opinion.

Ip Ching

I told Yip Man that I would do the house chores if he let me stay at his house. He said that I didn't have to do anything, just move in. I slept in the corridor in a canvas bed and ate whatever he did.

William Cheung

During one of his visits to Hong Kong in the mid-1960s, I ran into Bruce, and he said: "I have to train very hard to beat my opponents. So, I've come back to further my training in Wing Chun, and I hope to learn more of the dummy techniques from the old man (Yip Man). Hopefully, sifu will let me film him on 8mm so that I may show my students in the U.S. I'm on my way to see the old man now."

Hawkins Cheung

The teacher has to earn that loyalty and respect from the student. Loyalty is a two-way street but unfortunately, many instructors demand it from their students, but they do not give it back.

Emin Boztepe

I learned Wing Chun in Hong Kong from Sifu Lok Yiu from 1967 until 1971, and I served as an assistant instructor at one of Sifu Lok Yiu's schools.

Alan Lee

When I saw Yip Man stick hands with others, he was very relaxed and talked to his partner. I never once saw Yip Man take a step backward during chi sao.

Hawkins Cheung

Wing Chun punches, deflections and kicks can equally be deployed kneeling, standing, even lying on your back; it's only a matter of taking the tools and making them work freely.

Shaun Rawcliffe

"Chi Sau" is one of the many clever ways in which key attributes which may be required in a microsecond within the actual fight, can be loaded into the neural system and become a natural part of our arsenal of skill.

David Peterson

I personally do not believe that race or ethnicity has anything to do with advancement in kung fu. I believe it all comes down to your teacher's ability to teach, and the student's desire to work, train, and research what is taught.

Tony Massengill

Martial arts, like science, has no finish line, and there is always room for improvement. A good student understands that they have not mastered a technique and that they must keep practicing to improve.

William Kwok

Nowadays, the general public is much more sophisticated in regards to martial arts and is very aware of what works and what doesn't.

Randy Williams

I have been practicing the Hek Ki Boen system for more than three decades. My first Sifu, who I actually still learn from today, is Senior Grandmaster The Kang Hay.

Lin Xiang Fuk

There are many stories about Wing Chun weapons. Some people say the knives are arms' extensions; others say they are two different things. Wing Chun originally had no weapons.

Gorden Lu

The sifu-disciple relationship no longer exists. Kung fu has been commercialized, and the sifu has to accommodate the students.

Alan Lee

In contrast to other styles of kung-fu, wing chun forms are not always graceful or entertaining. The reason is that wing chun forms are designed to practice maneuvers.

Jim Lau

The Wing Chun system was designed to develop a person with no knowledge of martial art to eventually become a proficient fighter.

Hawkins Cheung

I began the research on *Gulao Wing Chun*, a style that was taught by Dr Leung Jan (1825-1894) after his retirement from Foshan and back to this hometown, Gulao. Gulao is a remote village in Heshan county in Southern China.

Donald Mak

Wing Chun is quite popular at present as we have practitioners from all over the world, but it should become more popular because it's an art that's very scientific, effective, and long-lasting.

Gary Lam

I have never wanted to tie myself to a specific organization because there are so many politics involved.

Alan Lamb

Bruce Lee used to write me, telling me how he was doing and the direction his research was taking. Sometimes he would ask for clarification of a wing chun technique or principle.

Wong Shun Leung

I try to stick to the "traditional" style. It was my goal to learn as much as I could about the style as Ip Man had practiced.

Samuel Kwok

Leung Sheung who was the Chef of the Kowloon Catering Union was the earliest student. He was the one who invited Yip Man to instruct the fellow workers in the Union Canteen.

Victor Kan

Yip Man was one of those masters who escaped from China to Hong Kong and my master helped him to teach for many years. The reason I have continued to learn from Sigung Tsui is to ensure that the purity of Wing Chun is retained so I can pass it on to my own students.

Jim Fung

In 1973, there were not many people in the early days. Wing Chun really was new to the West. Karate was popular. Some people loved Wing Chun and saw the value in its concepts. A lot of people found the art difficult.

Francis Fong

Most Westerners expect to line up and be given guided training with clear instruction and encouragement. The traditional Chinese way is to show them a simple skill and expect them to go off and practice, motivating themselves, or working one-on-one with more senior classmates with only limited interaction with the teacher.

David Peterson

I was introduced to Sifu Ho Kam Ming by another school friend of mine. He stopped training a short time after I started. Sifu Ho Kam Ming was my first and only teacher.

Augustine Fong

Thousands of years ago, the Chinese already knew that nothing stayed the same forever. They wrote the book "I-Ching," which means "the way of change." So, the "pure" always evolves.

Chung Kwok Chow

Throughout my years as a teacher, I have felt it necessary to keep up to date with teaching methodologies and perhaps more importantly, I have devised new ways to cater for the ever-changing needs of my students.

Shaun Rawcliffe

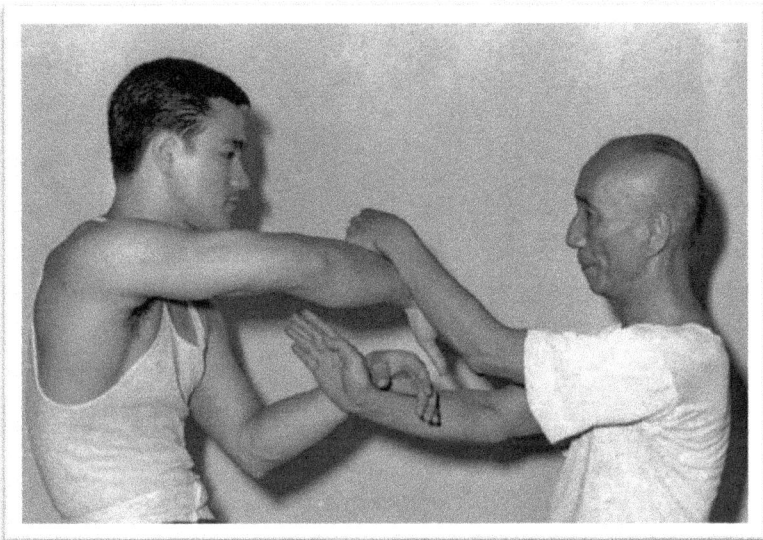

One thing I must say is that many come out of the woodwork with secret family systems which claim to be "original" or the most "traditional". Often these claims are just a form of puffery, based on greed or ignorance.

Robert Chu

Wing Chun, at least as far as "Wong Shun Leung system" is concerned, has only one goal—to develop truly effective personal combat skills. It is not a sporting, fitness, demonstration or meditative system.

David Peterson

The standard of Wing Chun in Europe is very high. In the United States the level is very inconsistent. Some are good, but many are not.

Ip Ching

In the early '50s, Yip Man began accepting formal students. Wong Shun Leung and myself were both swimmers. Wong Shun was practicing a different kung fu style.

William Cheung

There is an old Chinese saying that in real fighting, you must have three points: courage, strength, and technique. Technique comes last unless you have superior timing to deliver techniques.

Hawkins Cheung

In the early years I was only interested in fighting and being physically fit, in top physical condition, but due to personal problems with my parents and being always targeted by racial conflicts I needed to find a mental balance for my inner peace.

Emin Boztepe

The balance between physical and philosophical training is crucial for the improvement of the martial artist, and I stress the importance of cultivating a strong sense of culture and humility, which I refer to as martial virtues.

William Kwok

Training, teaching, and learning is a never-ending process of discovery, consolidation, and reappraisal.

Shaun Rawcliffe

I have been practicing Martial Arts for more than 40 years. My master is Sigung Tsui Sheung Tin, who was one of Yip Man's three closed-door students - the others being Leung Sheung and Lok Yiu.

Jim Fung

I started to learn Wing Chun when I was 15 years old. I learned Wing Chun from my father, Master Lo Man Kam, who is Wing Chun grandmaster Ip Man's nephew.

Gorden Lu

I trained in hung gar under Yee Chi Wai (Frank Yee). Yee is the successor to the Tang Fong system of hung gar, and I studied the major forms and weaponry of this system with him.

Robert Chu

A master can only be a master today. You can't tell what the future is, as the situation may change. You can only be a master up to the present. An individual has to develop, continue with his own research and grow every day.

Hawkins Cheung

Wing Tsun is distinctive because we use efficiency of motion, with techniques that follow the fastest and shortest path possible. We follow the centerline theory and avoid showy movements that other traditional styles may have.

Carson Lau

After I immigrated to the United States, I met Sifu Duncan Leung in 1975. Sifu Duncan Leung also was a private disciple of Sifu Yip Man; he helped me with further training, and together we taught Wing Chun.

Alan Lee

Whenever things are not working elsewhere in one's training, returning to the forms is generally the very best way to both identify and correct the problem.

David Peterson

I believe all systems have something to offer. Different people are drawn to different aspects of the arts. I do not think different styles are necessarily important other than for their appeal to the differing taste of the individual practitioner.

Tony Massengill

Certain instructors place more emphasis on actual combat applications, while others stress the more spiritual or artistic aspects of a system.

Randy Williams

Culturally, Taiwan, Hong Kong, and China still have many Kung Fu schools that are following the tradition. Most people and potential students know learning Martial Arts takes years and not everyone can be good or a master.

Gorden Lu

Chinese kung fu is an ancient art with a history dating back thousands of years. Some foreigners may first believe kung fu is mysterious or even strange, but if a sifu can properly explain the art to a student, there should be no real difficulty.

Alan Lee

After my graduation from college, I devoted a lot of my time and effort into professional teaching, training, researching, and promoting the true value of this ancient art.

Jim Lau

Smaller guys like Sigung Yip Man and Sifu Wong Shun Leung easily could overpower guys almost twice their size.

Gary Lam

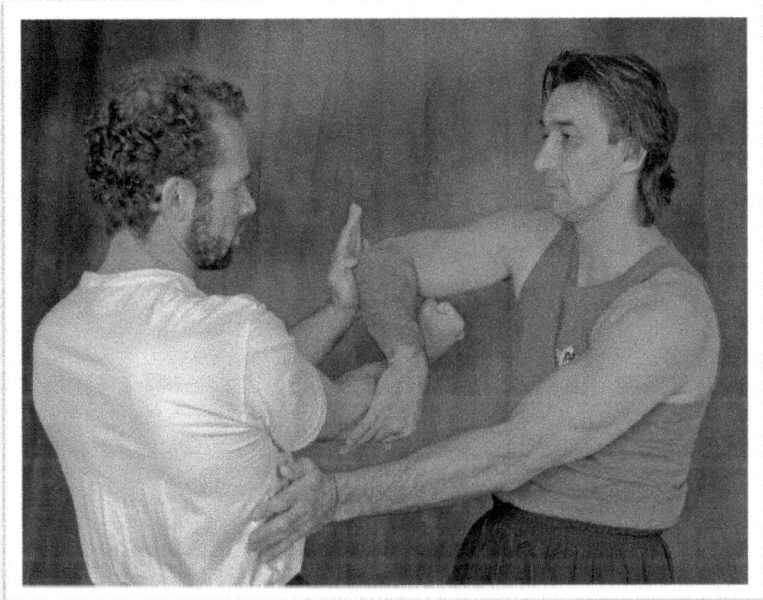

I think that Sifu Keith Kernspecht is the most organized and best wing chun teacher in Europe. He has so much knowledge about the martial arts in general, as well as knowledge about highly scientific methods for building up body strength, technique, and special conditioning exercises specifically for martial artists.

Alan Lamb

HISTORY

Learning Wing Chun was not easy for me at first, as I had previous training in other martial arts that had made some areas of my body tense and inflexible, thus making it difficult for me to execute some of the techniques in Wing Chun.

William Kwok

I taught Bruce Lee privately and also watched him train under Yip Man at the school. William Cheung introduced Bruce Lee to the wing chun system. Bruce trained and studied wing chun from me for over one-and-a- half years.

Wong Shun Leung

Yip Man selected me as a private disciple, and I trained under him for approximately two years. I learned from Sifu Yip Man during the late years of his life.

Alan Lee

My Wing Chun changed when I studied with Grandmaster Ip Chun, especially when I traveled around with him over a period of many years.

Samuel Kwok

In the mid 1950's Bruce was a very active teenager. He learned a bit here and a bit there in several different styles of martial arts. Until one day when he practiced some Ving Tsun, he was so impressed that he looked for the best instructor and he went to Yip Man to learn.

Victor Kan

In the late 1940s, when the Communists banned Martial Arts in China, some masters took their skills overseas. Most of those masters are now dead and it is arguable that the "pure styles" died with them.

Jim Fung

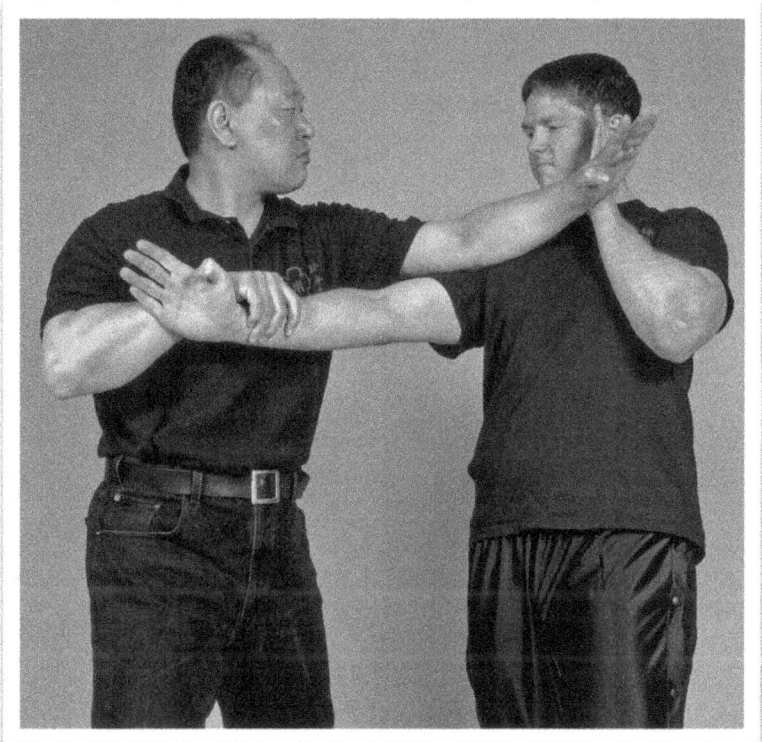

When I was 12 years old, I got involved in both Judo and Tae Kwon Do in two separate academies. The YMCA in Hong Kong offered Judo classes taught by Sensei Riki Hashimoto. I also joined a TKD school. I studied both Judo and TKD for three years. At that time, my friend Jason Lau brought me to his Wing Chun classes. He introduced me to Sifu Jiu Wan's school in Hong Kong

Francis Fong

My master, Wong Shun Leung, was strict with his students' training. In addition to understanding the forms, we had to practice sparring techniques and also engage in all-around training such as timed running and hitting the sandbag.

Kim Man Chan

I started training when I was 11 and against the wishes of my mother who was not very happy with the idea of me learning and training in Kung Fu. In fact, she didn't find out until the time I decided to move to the USA!

Augustine Fong

I love training WT and I hope that I will be able to do it for the rest of my life. The way I train will change as I grow older but that's okay. I can't wait to see the next generations of WT students flourish and take the system out into the world.

Thommy L. Boehlig

I also went to Hong Kong and Taiwan visited the elders of the system, including Wong Shun Leung, Tsui Sheung Tien, Lo Man Kam, Koo Sang and others. I also studied with William Cheung for a while. So my grounding is based mostly on the Yip Man system.

Robert Chu

I wanted to focus on a martial art that empowered smaller individuals to fight against larger opponents in real-life situations. I re-discovered Wing Chun, exploring various schools while still practicing Taekwon-do.

William Kwok

As long as the practitioner is alive, they have the opportunity to increase their understanding of Kung Fu. So I feel that I will continue to understand better as time passes.

Ip Ching

When you test your techniques on someone you don't know, you experience a different feeling than when training with your friends. If you discover through your own experience, it's much better than relying on another's experience.

Hawkins Cheung

The scientific approach to training and fighting is better than ever; there are more practitioners around the world than ever before, but this growth also brings other negative aspects. The old relationship teacher-student is being lost; money is the reason to teach, not love for the art. I guess like in everything else in life, expansion brings good and bad things at the same time.

Emin Boztepe

Particularly in the early years when Sifu began teaching at the VTAA Sifu's such as Wong Shun Leung, Lok Yiu, Tsui Sheung Tin, Leung Ting, Ip Ching and Siu Yuk Men would come and visit and I would have ample opportunity to discuss Wing Chun with them.

Shaun Rawcliffe

I really wanted to finish learning the system, so I wrote to the Hong Kong Martial Arts Association, and they put me in touch with Sifu Koo Sang who agreed to accept me as a student.

Alan Lamb

What we do is about personal protection concepts, or close-quarters combat, rather than the term self-defense which I personally do not like to use.

David Peterson

The only person who ever taught "a pure, authentic version of any system was the founder of that system; everyone else has changed it in some way, even if they didn't intend to make changes.

Tony Massengill

When I was beginning, it was very difficult to find anything about wing chun in print. There were few books in English and videos weren't born yet.

Randy Williams

Different styles of Kung Fu are here to represent a country or a region's culture, history and faith. In a broad sense, they are a guideline of disciplines, philosophy and spirituality.

Gorden Lu

Martial arts continue to improve as each generation competes against other styles. Without such interaction, you are stuck doing only your own games.

Alan Lee

I think different styles are good for kung fu in general. It allows people with different backgrounds to choose and compare which styles suit them better.

Gary Lam

At the age of 20 I immigrated to the U.S. to join my family. Settling in Los Angeles, I attended Pasadena City College where I began teaching wing chun as a means of arousing local interest and perfecting my own talents.

Jim Lau

Wong's style of kung-fu, siu lum-ji, was the parent system of wing chun. He had been a friend of Yip Man, and they had exchanged many ideas with each other.

Alan Lamb

My father had friends who practiced wing chun. One of them was a man named Chan Wah Sun. He would always tell me how good his teacher, Yip Man, was. I didn't believe him, so I decided to go to Yip Man's school and challenge him.

Wong Shun Leung

I met Bruce in intermediate school; he had been expelled from the famous European LaSalle Intermediate School to the Eurasian Francis Xavier Intermediate School which I attended. I used to make fun of him and call him "Bad Boy" because he was expelled.

Hawkins Cheung

I would have loved trained with Bruce Lee but the Wing Chun he and his group of students trained back then was drastically different to what I look for in WT today.

Thommy L. Boehlig

I furthered my studies with Grandmaster Ip Chun, who taught me the Wooden Dummy form and all the other Wing Chun forms in great detail.

Samuel Kwok

Six months after I started training, the late Bruce Lee joined the school. As a Si-hing I was told to help Bruce with his basic training. In fact, I spent a lot of time with him on the first form Sil Lim Tao, the little idea.

Victor Kan

Teaching other students is also an excellent means of sharpening techniques and keeping the mind open to different aspects of theory.

Jim Fung

Back in the 1950s, Yip Man trained us to fight, not be technicians. Because we were so young, we didn't understand the concepts or theories.

Hawkins Cheung

I got involved in a lot of different martial arts. I studied Wushu with my cousin in the U.S. and I studied Kali/Escrima and JKD Concepts under Guro Dan Inosanto, Muay Thai under Ajarn Chi Sirisute, Brazilian Jiu-Jitsu with the Machado brothers, Pentjak Silat, Savate, Shooto, and Tai Chi.

Francis Fong

Sifu Ho Kam Ming used to take Yip Man to the Hospital and stay with him. Grandmaster Yip Man gave him the responsibility of teaching private students when he couldn't do it for any reason.

Augustine Fong

There are many schools of wing chun. There's Yip Man, Yuen Kay Shan, Gu Lao, Pao Fa Lien, Chi Sim Weng Chun, Pan Nam and others. Of course, the best known is the school of Yip Man, and within it, there are many branches based on what the first-generation students of Yip Man interpreted.

Robert Chu

I don't believe there are any pure systems. I believe every system evolves somewhat with each person who learns it.

Ip Ching

On a personal level, going to Hong Kong to train was essential for me. I learned so much and gained a huge appreciation about Wing Chun, trained with some awesome people and learnt so much, but that was back in 1989 when Wing Chun was still hard to find, and a good teacher even harder.

Shaun Rawcliffe

The two weapons of the system, on the surface at least, would seem irrelevant in the modern world. After all, how often would one be carrying around a pole over nine feet long, or a pair of rather large meat cleavers?

David Peterson

An old proverb of wing chun says that its techniques are "limitless in their application." That means if you can think of it and it works, it's an application.

Randy Williams

In late 2006 Master Samuel Kwok asked me to write the book "Mastering Wing Chun - The Keys to Ip Man's Kung Fu". It was produced as a co-written project with Master Kwok. I wrote the book and Master Kwok flew in for the photos. I am very grateful to Master Kwok for giving me the opportunity to write the book.

Tony Massengill

When Yip Man taught me, he emphasized this scientific nature of Wing Chun and how there was a scientific reason for all of Wing Chun's details. He guided me to reach an understanding of these things, but he expected me to earn this knowledge through careful study and research.

Alan Lee

Ip Man was a police detective prior to teaching Wing Chun; because of his job function, he improved his Martial Arts skills as related to what he was doing. That's why Ip Man styles of Wing Chun also have some joint lock and take down techniques. But when Ip Man was teaching Wing Chun, he still followed the same curriculums and Wing Chun principles as he learned.

Gorden Lu

The system I train is too complex and extensive to really be mastered. The longer I train - and I have been practicing for more than 30 years—the more I realize how much room for improvement there is.

Thommy L. Boehlig

I made what eventually turned into a close friendship, as well as an ongoing learning relationship, with one of master Yip Man's first and most capable students, Sifu Wong Shun Leung.

Jim Lau

Although I believe the basics and foundation of Wing Chun remain the same, it definitely has evolved for the better as I gained more experience.

Gary Lam

Once I was supposed to go with Sifu Koo Sang to the cemetery to sweep Yip Man's grave as a sign of respect. However, I misunderstood what time we were supposed to meet at the school, and when I got there, he was already gone.

Alan Lamb

Bruce said that his father would support him and pay for his expenses in the U.S., but he wanted to be independent. To make money on the side, he said he would teach Wing Chun. I replied that he didn't have much to teach at that time; we had both only learned up to the second Wing Chun form, chum kiu, and 40 movements on the dummy.

Hawkins Cheung

I started learning Wing Chun from Lee Sing, who was a student of Grandmaster Ip Man. Lee Sing was my first Wing Chun teacher, and it was he who introduced me to Grandmaster Ip Chun in 1978.

Samuel Kwok

Yip Man named Sigung Tsui the "King of Sil Lum Tao" and I believe the strong foundation he developed is the reason why he became so highly skilled in Wing Chun.

Jim Fung

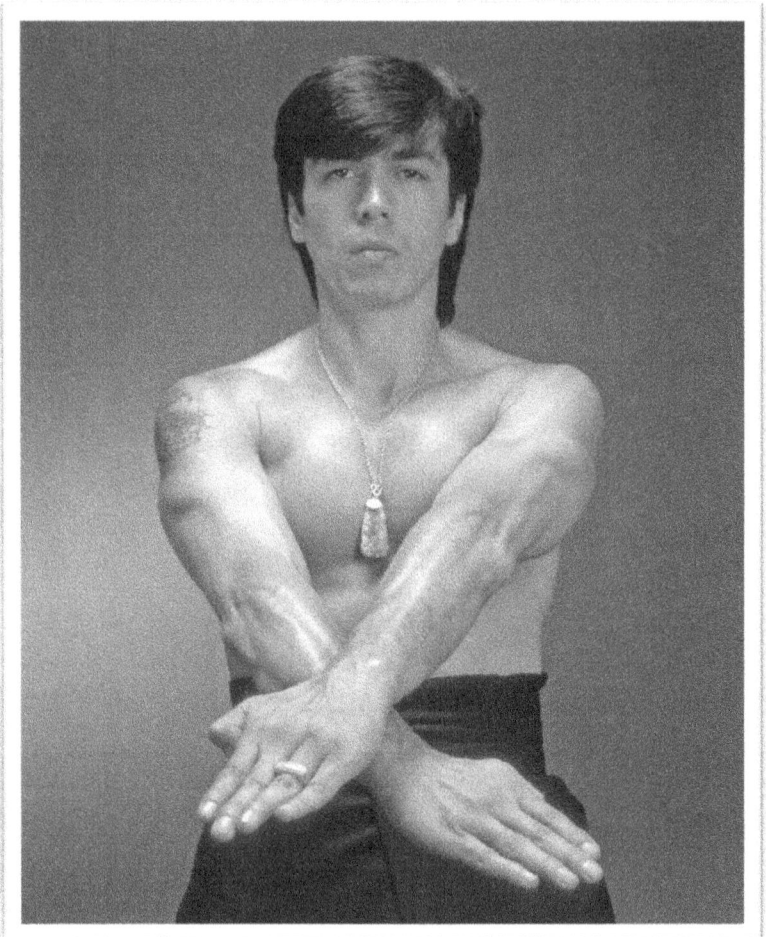

The key to learning is to be patient, students have to learn to replace old habits with new learned skills and the transition between the two is difficult one.

Shaun Rawcliffe

One day after the class my friend took me to see a middle-aged bald gentleman who was teaching at the school. I remember that he was wearing the traditional Chinese long dress. He looked at me and said "You are rather big and well-built for your age. I will call you Big Boy." Everybody laughed at his remarks. I later found out that Grandmaster Yip Man always liked to address his students by their nicknames.

Victor Kan

My Sifu Ho Kam Ming spent all his life training and studying the art of Wing Chun. He was one of the very few who actually finished the Wing Chun training under the supervision of the legendary Yip Man.

Augustine Fong

I later on in my training I went to seek out Master Hawkins Cheung in wing chun and have been with him since 1988. He is truly a master and an honorable man, and it is his methods that I primarily use.

Robert Chu

I began training with my father as a child, and continued training when my father went to Hong Kong. I resumed training with my father when I joined him in Hong Kong in 1962.

Ip Ching

In Wing Chun, the term "centerline" not only refers to the line in fighting, it also refers to your mind, the things you do, the problems you solve, the way that you live your life.

Hawkins Cheung

Many practitioners of quite different systems have been drawn to Wing Chun and have found that its direct approach and logical methods are very appealing, compared with what they have previously studied.

David Peterson

I had the good fortune to have the opportunity to training directly with Ip Chun and Ip Ching through travels to Hong Kong and Foshan, China with Samuel Kwok. I spent quite a bit of time with Ip Ching in researching the system during the time I was writing the book "Mastering Wing Chun – The Keys to Ip Man's Kung Fu".

Tony Massengill

I had to work very hard to develop certain skills, and still do. Plus, I had a language barrier to overcome. My Sifu wasn't going to learn English anytime soon, so he made me learn at least some basic Chinese before he'd even consider taking me on as a student.

Randy Williams

During those years of learning, practicing, training, and developing I did develop my personal style in the system. So when I use and teach the art, I have a broader experience and background than other people.

Gorden Lu

Many people have heard of Sifu Yip Man's incredible physical prowess and martial arts knowledge. However, very few people got the opportunity to experience his teaching skills outside of class.

Alan Lee

At 14, I started my study of the wing chun system. Like most other boys of that age, I did not understand the significance of such an experience. The seeds of my appreciation for wing chun as an intelligent and practical art were, however, planted.

Jim Lau

I practiced two years with Sifu Lok Yiu and later with Sifu Wong Shun Leung for more than two decades. I consider myself very fortunate to have trained under the legendary Wong Shun Lung.

Gary Lam

All martial arts are unique, though obviously there are a limited way the body's skeleton can move, but I see Wing Chun as the ugly runt of the litter; it's not aesthetically pleasing, not classy nor particularly elegant, but fights dirty and hard!

Shaun Rawcliffe

I trained and compared fighting styles for many years with fellow students skilled in various styles of Martial Arts, some of whom had already reached senior level. The more I learned about other systems, the more impressed I became with the Wing Chun system.

Jim Fung

I was introduced to the Wing Chun White Crane Fuijien Style. Master Cheng Man Lung—he was the full contact fighting champion in Canton (during the 1980s)—was very powerful because of his Dim Mak skill, and he trained with a bucket full of granite rocks.

Samuel Kwok

My Wing Tsun journey has been blessed with two beloved teachers: my Sifu Cheng Cheun Fun and my Si-Bak Leung Ting, who is also the Si-Hing of my Sifu.

Carson Lau

When I was young, street fighting, violence and crime were common in Hong Kong. As I grew up in such a troubled society, I felt that I needed to learn some form of martial art to protect myself and my family.

Victor Kan

Kung Fu training often emphasizes the development of the mind, body, and spirit as a unified whole. This holistic approach is rooted in traditional Chinese philosophy, particularly Taoism and Confucianism. Taoism emphasizes the concept of balance and harmony, both within the individual and with the natural world. Confucianism emphasizes the importance of personal morality and ethics, as well as the cultivation of virtues such as wisdom, courage, and compassion.

Mohammed Ince

Joseph was a disciple of Sifu Lee Sing, who had also studied with Yip Man, and they were teaching a mainland version of wing chun. It was interesting to experience a different form of wing chun.

Alan Lamb

All of the founders of the above martial arts must have had some training elsewhere in order to create their system, so only people under that rigid thought of "lineage" try to be pure. Ed Parker said it best—"When pure fist meets pure flesh—that's pure.

Robert Chu

When you take into account the fact that Wing Chun, by and large, is concept-driven, as opposed to any definite physical attribute, the differences in physical ability are more or less nonexistent.

David Peterson

As a martial artist, one must stand on his own credit, not his master's. When I teach Wing Chun tools to my students, I coach them to find which way best fits their character.

Hawkins Cheung

Historically, the movements and the benefits of using the Pole as a weapon were to increase the fighting range and to benefit from increased angular momentum, and therefore power, when striking or blocking, which really has little direct or practical bearing on improving street combat skills.

Shaun Rawcliffe

People simply like to place things in baskets for ease of discussion, so "Kung Fu" and "Wushu" have become a victim of this trend to the extent that many people now believe that all Chinese Martial Arts are for sport and exercise, having no real combat merit – nothing could be further from the truth!

David Peterson

Since ancient times, kung fu has been a combat art used to defend the homeland and fight enemies.

Kim Man Chan

I began training in Wing Chun and getting my introduction into the system under the instruction of Shiu Hung (Duncan) Leung. I trained with him steadily until I began a career in the police department in 1982. I trained sporadically from that time until 1984.

Tony Massengill

Because Ving Tsun is a simple, easy-to-learn martial art that does not require a significant amount of energy, it is full of academic value and practicality.

Kim Man Chan

I learned from my father who is an expert on the short bridge Wing Chun, I also learned from my Kung Fu uncle sifu Duncan Leung and who is an expert on long bridge Wing Chun.

Gorden Lu

My first teacher was Sifu George Yau Chu from Hong Kong. I met him when he walked by and stayed to watch while I was hitting and kicking a bag in my garage. He was my neighbor in LA Chinatown. Coincidentally, so was Sifu Ted Wong.

Randy Williams

The word "Master" is one that is too easily bandied about in the modern era, largely because of a mistranslation of the Eastern terms for teachers of the Martial Arts.

David Peterson

Developed during a period when self-defense was literally a matter of life or death, the practice of the Baat Cham Dao form today is not learnt or practiced for street practical application, but to enhance the practitioners understanding of Wing Chun theory, footwork, and energy usage.

Shaun Rawcliffe

Teaching Wing Chun has changed tremendously from the old times.

Alan Lee

Sifu Joseph Cheng was running a class in London's Chinatown, and I practiced at his school for a year before leaving for Hong Kong.

Alan Lamb

My interest in Wing Chun continued in 1968 when a guy who played basketball showed me the Sim Lao Tao form; however, I was not very impressed at his demonstration of the form.

Samuel Kwok

Eventually, I began training under the Ip Family method under the Ip Chun—Ip Ching—Samuel Kwok lineage, where I earned a Master Level certification in 2005.

Tony Massengill

Back then, the teaching methods were more traditional than they are today. I learned easily by attending three to four times a week, but sometimes it was dull. We practiced the same techniques for days on end. It was tedious at times, but it strengthened my foundation.

Carson Lau

I learned Wing Chun fighting techniques casually on and off for a few years before commencing private classes seriously with Sigung Tsui. At the time, Sigung Tsui was conducting most of Yip Man's classes.

Jim Fung

I trained primarily in Shaolin, hung gar, and wing chun kuen in my youth. Despite all my cross training, I view my personal style as wing chun. I practice and teach tai ji quan also, but I feel wing chun is more closely suited to my personality.

Robert Chu

When Yip Man faced a larger opponent, his skill was so high that he would shut off his opponent's move or never let it start. When you're old, you have to adapt this way to survive. Yip Man's skill in the 1950s was the epitome of sensitivity; he could immediately read his opponent's intention.

Hawkins Cheung

In 1994 summer, I followed my father's instruction and traveled to the U.S. to study another style of Wing Chun from his junior Kung Fu brother Sifu Duncan Leung, the disciple of the grandmaster.

Gorden Lu

PHILOSOPHY

In order to develop Wing Chun skills within Chi Sao or in application training it is vital to train with, not on, your partner.

Shaun Rawcliffe

Martial arts was not only a physical training for me, but a holistic experience. It helped me explore my mental and emotional boundaries and further my personal development. Through the hard training and challenges I faced, I developed strength, stamina and self-confidence.

Mohammed Ince

Martial arts became more than just a physical activity for me. I applied my Kung Fu in everyday life, in the way I spoke, felt, thought, wrote, planned events & business. For me, kung fu is my way of life.

Carson Lau

PHILOSOPHY

Society seems to undergo a tremendous change nowadays and students don't seem to want to suffer and endure repetition after repetition in order to achieve mastery anymore.

Thommy L. Boehlig

In Wing Chun, you give up your arm's power, you will get better body-arm-leg unity and thus a better utilization of your body mechanics. This is an example of how Wing Chun's concepts apply to our daily life problems.

Donald Mak

Each style has its unique set of techniques and training methods that serve specific purposes. It was only after training with my Sifu that I was able to fully comprehend my own needs and establish new goals for my personal martial arts practice.

William Kwok

Wing Chun isn't to everyone's taste, and that is to be expected, but the person who appreciates logic and science is sure to find Wing Chun fascinating and may well be drawn to take up its practice.

David Peterson

Wing Chun training emphasizes response to situations by reflex and feeling, rather than with one specific technique against another technique, which is what you find with many other kung fu styles.

Alan Lee

A successful martial artist requires a significant amount of dedication, including time, patience, and hard work.

Kim Man Chan

Anything that improves health and fitness is good. I just warn the students to consider their ultimate goal. Is it looking like Mr. or Mrs. America or being to apply their skills with flow, speed, power and accuracy. If their goal is the second, then I warn them against "heavy" weight training.

Tony Massengill

In Wing Chun, some things don't really need to be original due to the personal experiences, but something should be the same: the basic principles.

Gorden Lu

Cross-training has already proven to improve a fighter's effectiveness in a competitive environment. But in terms of keeping an art systematic and preserving its original essence, there have to be dinosaurs like myself, who keep the arts separate and to some degree pure and original.

Randy Williams

When you have learned your art inside out and spent enough time, you begin to move within the context of the art—therefore, everything you do is training.

Robert Chu

Mixing styles is more of a "modern approach." Where it focuses on collecting all technical knowledge that works, this is by all means "Using all ways as the way."

Lin Xiang Fuk

PHILOSOPHY

There's an old Chinese saying, "the art always passes to the people who have fate with that art." The Wing Chun system has been out there for years. The system does not change much, but people change.

Gorden Lu

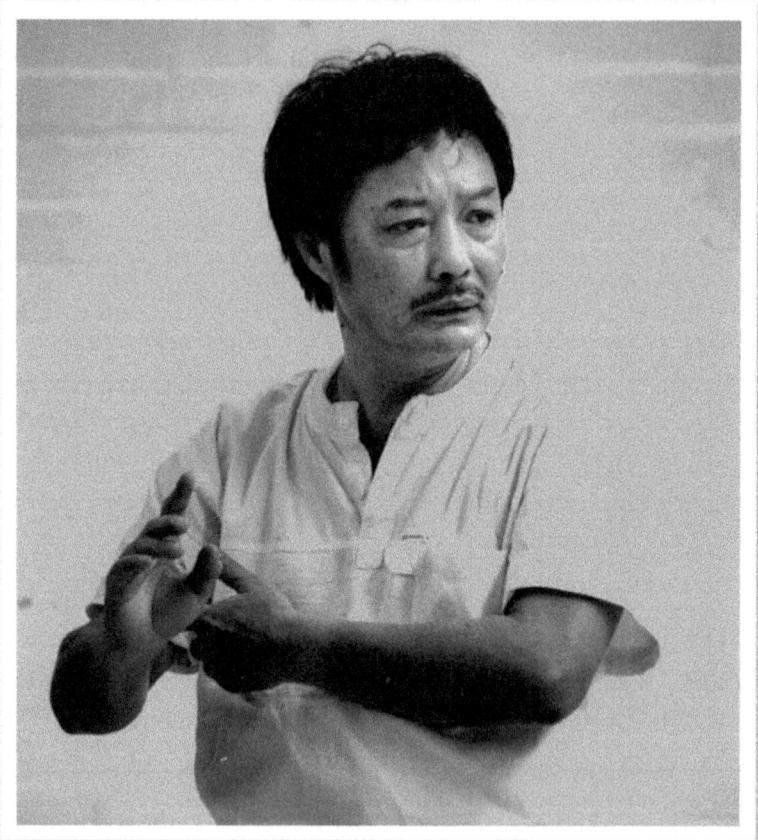

A successful student must have a hardworking attitude, determination and dedication to train diligently and consistently, common sense to analyze how to improve his kung fu, and open-mindedness to accept other ideas.

Alan Lee

Although wing chun emphasizes individuality as the ultimate ideal, it is impossible to learn the art by oneself, or through a book. Just as a child needs guidance in learning to walk, so too does the novice need instruction in learning to fight.

Jim Lau

Most kung fu styles rely on physical strength and condition. They make their fist, palm, and even the head tougher by subjecting them to rigorous training.

Gary Lam

Don't risk your life against an armed aggressor just because you study Kung Fu. Accepting a meaningless fight like these when you can escape it means that you are a fool posing like a hero!

Leung Ting

If one learns martial arts' skills, but does not pay attention to fighting, then they are neglecting the essence to pursue trifles—since martial arts are not just physical exercises.

Wong Shun Leung

Wing Chun Kung Fu is a way of life, I think it teaches you to work hard and achieve your goals, not to give up easily and to do a lot of thinking—to use your cognitive abilities during your Wing Chun training and in everyday life.

Samuel Kwok

Health and exercise is not a priority (you do not need to be a super athlete to perform Wing Chun), nor is tradition, if what you mean by that to be bowing, fancy uniforms and rituals.

David Peterson

I aim to enhance the way I present my teachings so that my students can understand the concepts and principles of the system better. The students who are patient and don't hurry into learning too quickly are more proficient in the art.

Carson Lau

When we look at how most masters teach, we find out that their method is based on learning by rote, on the drill-like instilling of habits by repetition. This is entirely out of kilter with Chan-Buddhism, which is about presence of mind and also spontaneity.

Keith R. Kernspecht

Nowadays, students frequently ask to be taught more advanced forms before they have learned the first. They seem to think that the more forms they learn in a short time, the better they will become.

Victor Kan

Wing Chun is a very useful self-defense system but while it is easy to learn, it is very hard to master. Like learning anything, you must be committed and open-minded.

Jim Fung

Motivation is internal. I love what I am doing. I learn different things every day I teach, especially from my students, my associates, and my family.

Francis Fong

Conquering the physical art of the art heightens your own personal internal growth. Find the universal law of personal truth and kindness through the art of Wing Chun.

Augustine Fong

Remember that these days, the majority of people do not study Martial Arts because their survival depends upon it, so this is why many people choose to study forms of the Martial Arts (Martial Sports) that appeal to their need to engage in physical exercise.

David Peterson

Sport and real self-protection do not coexist. They are like "security" and "free access." The more you have of one, the less you have of the other. If a building is "totally secure," there is NO free access. If there is "free access," there is NO real security. Sport and self-protection work in much the same way.

Kim Man Chan

The best way to learn is to take the Wing Chun out of the classroom and increase the variables and unknown s whilst still making it a training and learning experience.

Shaun Rawcliffe

Students must train in a way to develop not only technique, but the ability to apply technique. In Wing Chun, we use Chi Sao for much of this training.

Ip Chun

The inventors of the system never had to consider combat against the many modern and non-Chinese arts that a fighter may encounter today, such as Thai boxing, shoot-fighting, Brazilian jiu-jitsu and sambo just to name but a few.

Randy Williams

Every martial art has its own charm and appeal. Ving Tsun, in particular, is known for its practicality and effectiveness in self-defense.

Tony Massengill

Unless these foundation skills and concepts are understood and trained consistently, progress in Wing Chun is slow and the chances of reaching a high level of proficiency unlikely.

David Peterson

Kung fu actually means "a skill from practicing." During the practice, you would have many hardships, but you should keep going rather than giving up too soon.

Chung Kwok Chow

Wing Chun training is different for each person; by not influencing or flavoring the training focus, I hope to give each student the opportunity to take from it what they need.

Shaun Rawcliffe

True martial arts deal with a life-or-death situation and it also looks to heal the body, mind, and spirit. Too many are practicing to be brawlers or fighters, but a true martial artist develops the soul of a Jun Zi—Confucius' idea of a nobleman—not necessarily in prestige or rank, but rather in character.

Robert Chu

I learned very quickly that all of the "sport-based" tournament Martial Arts do not stand up to the realities of the street. From that point until today, I have been standing on my soapbox and preaching the importance of "reality-based" training in the Martial Arts.

Tony Massengill

It is important that we maintain proper standards if the Wing Chun system is to survive. It would be very sad to see this system become extinct after just a few generations.

Ip Ching

My philosophy of fighting is that if you can avoid a fight, do it. I don't recommend that anyone fight. But if you have to do it, watch your opponent's nearest elbow.

William Cheung

Good Wing Chun is like playing billiards, you must always look for the next shot. Make your opponent follow you, if you are fast, make him catch up to you.

Hawkins Cheung

Teaching and developing Wing Chun Kung Fu is a very personal thing. It does not depend on the color or race of the student but totally rely on the built and the learning ability of the student.

Stephen Chan

In Wing Chun, we learn how to fight by the principle; we see scientific effects in the system and the movements that we practice use the natural reaction.

Gorden Lu

The most important point in my teaching method is to be able to bring out the Martial Arts interest from the student. If I can make the students interested to learn kung fu, then they will automatically want to learn more and devote more time to practice. In this way, they will have the chance to become proficient in the arts.

Au Yeung

One of the elements of wing chun centerline theory is moderation. Much like one uses a compass to check his direction, if one knows moderation it is safer to deviate and still find your way back.

Jim Lau

Teaching too fast can confuse the student. Thus, I always educate my students to "learn better, not only more."

Carson Lau

Nobody will do forms or sticky hands with you in a street fight. If a practitioner never actually applies what he has learned from the art, what you have is just a "fighting hero talking behind the desk."

Alan Lee

I think that the origin or nationality of an instructor doesn't matter! It matters if the instructor has a good education in that particular art and did he overcome his personal physical and mental weaknesses.

Emin Boztepe

Supplementary exercises may develop muscle groups that are detrimental or antagonists to the muscle group required to drive a powerful punch.

Shaun Rawcliffe

Don't take yourself too seriously and enjoy your training—it's okay to have fun when you train—no need to act like you're on a divine mission.

David Peterson

I believe it is important to be compassionate and respectful. Real kung fu is real power. It is the power to injure another human being. With power comes responsibility. Without compassion, one with these skills can do more harm than good.

Tony Massengill

I would advise a student to pick his style and teacher with the utmost care and attention. You must weigh certain factors and decide which are the most important to you.

Randy Williams

Moreover, this martial art has embraced a great deal of Chinese culture with respect to the philosophy of life. Learning and practicing Wing Chun can help to some problems in our daily life.

Donald Mak

My generation of WT students and the one before us drove and flew to faraway places frequently to get training from the best masters out there.

Thommy L. Boehlig

Kung Fu is about achievement with hard work. This should also cover your personal life and your family, as well as your career.

Lin Xiang Fuk

To get the most out of my private training sessions with my Sifu, I adopted the "empty your cup" philosophy, which required me to approach my training with an open mind and without any preconceived notions or biases from previous martial arts experiences.

William Kwok

The very best instruction comes from people who live and breathe Wing Chun. Lineage, training, background, and many years of instruction in Wing Chun are the most important.

Gorden Lu

I consider Wing Chun to be the best martial arts style. However, I believe most practitioners of our style are too proud.

Alan Lee

The muk yan jong is made from a tree trunk and has two wooden arms and a wooden leg, attached to resemble a man. This "hypothetical opponent" is probably the most advanced apparatus in existence for kung-fu training.

Jim Lau

The problem with sport-oriented programs is that they teach the student to react in a manner other than the way they will need to react in order to protect themselves in a violent street encounter.

Tony Massengill

PHILOSOPHY

The major drawbacks these days are lack of patience and not setting realistic goals. Wing Chun is not an art that can be mastered overnight because it's so in-depth.

Gary Lam

What I can say with certainty is that when I have taught women who were really motivated to learn, they learned the art and adapted to it much quicker than men.

Alan Lamb

I always encourage my students to participate in different competitions in the tournaments. I want them to understand what type of tournaments fit for them because this is very important.

Gorden Lu

We must always strive to make the training reality-based and to ensure that we are honest about the way that we train.

David Peterson

The notion of a pure Kung Fu style is false. There are many renowned names in the Yip Man lineage who trained under him. They all have their own understanding of what they learned.

Carson Lau

Each style of martial arts has a unique approach to fighting, so when these styles compete against each other, the practitioners adapt, learn, and improve their knowledge.

Alan Lee

Train hard but train hard under pressure. They are two different things. Pressure is the key factor that changes everything.

Leung Ting

There is an old Chinese saying that goes, "Courage first, strength second, and kung-fu third." To secure victory in a face-to-face fight with fist and kicks, one must be courageous. The courage comes from one's own self-cultivation and is one of the purposes of trials of skills.

Wong Shun Leung

Blindly ignoring the beauty of an effective technique simply because you were never shown it as a "classical" example of the principles of your style is cheating yourself and your style.

Randy Williams

I don't think being at a beginner level in a lot of systems makes you more proficient than having a depth of knowledge in a single system.

Tony Massengill

The process of learning and development is similar to the journey from crawling to walking, from walking to running, and finally to full speed running. It is a gradual process that requires patience, perseverance, and dedication.

Mohammed Ince

PHILOSOPHY

The more educated and pragmatic students of today care only very briefly about the names of one's instructors, conflicting claims concerning who is a master or successor of a style, or other such irrelevancies.

Jim Lau

In the past, certain acknowledged ancestors made additions and improvements to the system, and it is my belief that the system will have to be continually modified.

Randy Williams

The relationship of Chi Sao with the practical application of Wing Chun is best answered as follows: "To learn Wing Chun through the Chi Sao exercise, one can begin to understand the forms, and also realize what specialty of strength is needed, or indeed. not needed, in the distinct and subtle changes of each move".

Samuel Kwok

Anybody who has practiced Wing Tsun for many years should have developed sufficient means of self-defense. Things are quite different for those who have perhaps only been training for a few months. Yet it is precisely those who have a need for security.

Keith R. Kernspecht

Chinese martial arts are known for their relaxed, agile, and elastic movements, which are unique to the Chinese people.

Kim Man Chan

Novices do not know enough about Ving Tsun theory, footwork and stance to be able to use the dummy and must wait until they have more skill.

Victor Kan

Do whatever you feel is right. You should be able to motivate yourself to do whatever you need to do to be healthy. Try to improve yourself so you can enjoy what you are doing, and then to give back to help the next generation.

Francis Fong

PHILOSOPHY

I may not have been a "natural" at kung fu, my dedication to training and constant improving has helped me develop a deeper appreciation for martial arts and a greater respect for those who have dedicated themselves to mastering it.

William Kwok

Don't look or be worried by other people's progress. Focus on your own development. A good teacher never holds knowledge back from the student, but the student must show respect and dedication.

Augustine Fong

I believe the future of Wing Chun is very bright. The series of movies on my father have brought worldwide attention to Wing Chun. We now have instructors all over the world who are spreading the Wing Chun method.

Ip Chun

Kung fu is a sport when you use it in regulated competitions. It is an art when you practice it. It is a tradition if you study the history. It is a way of life when you think about it all of the time.

Chung Kwok Chow

Teachers shouldn't teach you theory, but rather they should teach you principles that work. Instructors shouldn't just teach techniques, but the concepts needed to create techniques. The difference is whether a person has gone through the experience or not.

Robert Chu

We can't stop people from teaching improper methods and poor standards. We can only ensure that our Wing Chun is of proper standard.

Ip Ching

You can discard and simplify when you already have something. Probably some people have oversimplified some things, and the art is getting too thin. Bruce had a lot of knowledge and there are certain things that won't work unless you have that amount of knowledge too.

William Cheung

I see Wing Chun as a system, rather than a style, because it is a complete, scientifically developed method of combat that utilizes a complete program of skills and concepts that are adaptable and interlocking—styles do not have the cohesion that a system has.

David Peterson

Don't fight it if you have too much to lose. If you must fight, you must destroy your opponent and not stop until he is defeated.

Hawkins Cheung

Wing Chun Kung Fu as an art suffered drastic changes throughout these last thirty or forty years to be a more lethal and effective martial art with an introduction to MMA.

Stephen Chan

I'm not a fan of MMA events. I understand the human (especially male) drive to compete with others. I've been there and I've done that. I also admire the physical and mental condition a lot of fighters are in. These guys are real athletes and I love that.

Thommy L. Boehlig

To understand the way other people practice is useful, as you can use it to improve and adapt it into your own training. This way enables you to always learn more and can constantly improve on what you've got.

Au Yeung

Be honest to yourself and train hard. I like people who dedicate themselves to whatever path they have chosen. Honestly it's an extremely important word for me and I try to show that in everything I do in life, not only in martial arts.

Emin Boztepe

Through training in Kung Fu, we learn not only fighting techniques, but also important life lessons. It teaches us discipline, perseverance, self-confidence, and respect. It strengthens our body and our mind and helps us to know ourselves better and to expand our limits.

Mohammed Ince

I utilize Wing Chun system short and long bridge fighting techniques in a more complete way and bring these other areas of experience to the table as well, so my students gain access to this more flexible approach.

Gorden Lu

The most important qualities for a student are a good personality, an open mind, a willingness to learn and dedication to put in the time and the practice required.

Shaun Rawcliffe

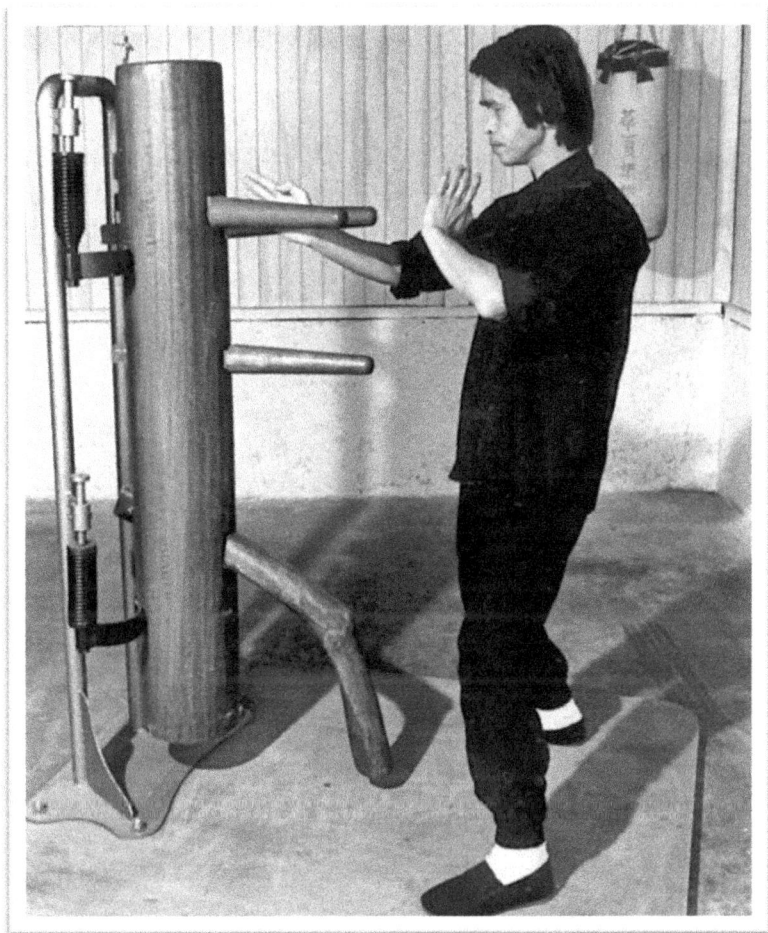

Perseverance, hard work, humility, a positive attitude towards others—these are all qualities that will take us far in our journey along the Martial Road.

David Peterson

No one ever wins a fight in the street. There is always a price to pay if you have to injure another human being. Even if you are totally in the right, you will likely have to hire an attorney to defend your actions in criminal and/or civil court.

Tony Massengill

If success for you means commercial success, then I would advise you to put out a good product, be it instruction, books, videos, or magazine articles. I can tell you from experience that you will have to look at that article and those photos for the rest of your life, so you better do the best you possibly can, or you'll regret it for many years to come.

Randy Williams

Talent is not something you are born with, but it is about how much experience you have. Sky is not even the limit.

Lin Xiang Fuk

Full-contact competition can be used to improve practical martial arts skills in a sporting context, but MMA can be seen as a life-and-death struggle and has gone beyond the realm of sports.

Kim Man Chan

We need to understand why and how this works this way because eventually all the Wing Chun knowledge that you are exposed to will build your own personal Wing Chun style.

Gorden Lu

Self-respect; self-confidence; self-defense; always aim high; never give up; be more humble; always work hard; be a better person in conduct and morals; carry on the knowledge of Wing Chun with dignity.

Alan Lee

The role of footwork in wing chun is the reason why there are few, if any, blocks in the system. The footwork is our way of blocking. Blocks are unnecessary when your opponent can't touch you.

Jim Lau

Some schools may focus on traditional training while others may focus on modern training & sparring from different styles. The most important thing is to have fun. If you don't enjoy what you love, you're doing it wrong.

Carson Lau

I have freely used my own common sense and experience to help me derive certain applications and principles of the system that are not as obvious as others, and to use these to help me deal with modern combat situations not encountered and therefore not considered by the founders of the system.

Randy Williams

I don't recommend that any of my students develop big muscles, as Wing Chun is not based on brute force. The other sports I'd probably recommend are running and swimming.

Gary Lam

The meaning of the practice of Kung Fu is that through focus, diligence, hard work and determination anyone can learn to do the seemingly impossible, develop skills that you didn't think possible and comfortably interact with others in a physical language with ease.

Shaun Rawcliffe

Most misconceptions arise from people who have never studied wing chun or those who have only studied a portion of the wing chun system, and whose knowledge is incomplete.

Alan Lamb

In my school's curriculum (sixteen levels in total), I incorporate and teach the two traditional "styles" comprising the *Ip Man* and *Gulao* lineages.

Donald Mak

You see a lot of people wanting to "Mix the BEST of each system" into one fighting method. But how do you know what the BEST of a system is until you have studied the system in depth.

Tony Massengill

Basic techniques are the ones we should use in real fights…therefore these "basic" techniques are the true secret of our training.

Leung Ting

I have to adapt my mentality to the country. Of course, the Chinese customs are different from the American or European, but the wing chun system is taught the same.

Wong Shun Leung

I suggest you find the right teacher, learn the basics in depth, learn the theory, and understand it and the core principles. Ask questions that will aid your understanding and train diligently, especially in Chi Sao.

Samuel Kwok

Theoretically, wing chun forms serve as a reference guide which articulates all the basic movements and fighting techniques within the context of the centerline.

Jim Lau

Traditionally, even after years of study, if your Sifu does not say you are good enough to teach or prove, you should not teach or open the school; the students will not disobey. This is also how the students show loyalty and respect to the Sifu, school and the art.

Gorden Lu

I wouldn't say that my personal Kung Ku has changed over the years, but it has certainly developed in the sense that I am now finding more efficient ways to use the system.

David Peterson

WT is not for the ring. It's not even for the street. It is a system of war designed to kill and to damage an opponent in the most vicious way. That's why in my eyes it has no business in the tournament world.

Thommy L. Boehlig

PHILOSOPHY

Siu Lim Tao is the first indication that Wing Tsun, which was originally a northern system according to Grandmaster Yip Man, is conceived as what we might call an internal style.

Keith R. Kernspecht

Muk Yan Jong is for toughening the arms and legs. In fact, this form actually teaches them how to move around an attacker effectively in a real combat situation, counter-attacking with ease and full body force.

Jim Fung

In Wing Chun, the weapons are an extension of the arms, but they are more harmful and can take someone's life in a conflict.

Alan Lee

The old way of learning and training is the best way. Simply because that in the 'old days', people relied completely on their Kung Fu skill to defend themselves and stop other people killing them!

Victor Kan

Wing Chun is not easy because you need a lot of patience, even as an adult. It is never too late to begin. Age doesn't matter. What does matter is what you think. It doesn't matter what other people say. It matters how you feel.

Francis Fong

In Wing Chung we use kicks to supplement and back up the hand techniques. They are also generally directed below the belt level and are well-timed and executed in close association with the upper body movements.

Augustine Fong

Currently, my teaching focuses on physical training to help students enhance their physical endurance and fitness. In order to truly understand the Wing Chun philosophy, both physical and analytical abilities are required.

Kim Man Chan

Conditioning is important to one's health. But in a real self-protection situation as opposed to a sporting contest, knowledge and skill are more important than conditioning.

Ip Ching

I believe each individual has their own meaning of Kung Fu. Some place more importance on health, some on self-defense, some on competition. I believe your approach can bring out what you want from Kung Fu.

Ip Chun

Different styles of Kung Fu are like different styles of painting. Different painting may tell you a different story, age, culture, the feeling, history, background, and emotional aspect of the artists.

Gorden Lu

To me, kung fu means a lot—including building my personality and values along with it. You also can use them to influence other people's lives, and I did it many times. There is no finish line for any knowledge.

Chung Kwok Chow

Kung fu is an art that requires serious dedication to perfection. Unfortunately, most people treat it like a hobby and practice it only part-time.

Alan Lee

The way most people practice is a sport, a recreation. I think martial arts are not a sport, but rather an art form. It is in a unique category. Martial arts is still the best name, rather than being classified as a sport.

Robert Chu

Conditioning is important to one's health. But in a real self-protection situation as opposed to a sporting contest, knowledge and skill are more important than conditioning.

Ip Ching

Bruce Lee found what was useful for him, and he used certain logical philosophy. I don't think the name "Jeet Kune Do" is that important.

William Cheung

I often compare Wing Chun to a gunfight—when the enemy fires at you, you immediately present the smallest target possible and return fire—you don't try to block the bullets!

David Peterson

The best Wing Chun players can combine both offense and defense simultaneously in one beat if offense and defense are separated, you're not adhering to Wing Chun principles.

Hawkins Cheung

From my point of view, different "styles" is equivalent to different forms of combat, and since we are all different in size, build, and mentality, we need a variety of "styles" to fulfill each different requirement. In addition, each "style" offers a slightly different way of training; it would be beneficial to be aware of all the different types if you want to achieve all-round training.

Au Yeung

I encourage my students to travel to Hong Kong or any other country. I truly believe this is the only way they can keep their mind open to others and help themselves to overcome their limitation of any kind of judgment you may have to make over another style or person.

Emin Boztepe

A fight or attack situation escalates very quickly and is a very fluid and volatile situation. The time from reception to disengagement can be a matter of seconds and the consequences can be terrible, potentially deadly.

Shaun Rawcliffe

Loyalty, honesty, and sincerity go a long way in earning the respect of one's teacher too, not to mention the respect of one's peers.

David Peterson

Today's Martial Artists have lost the element of respect. There is too much emphasis on sport. The Martial Arts were originally about eliminating the ego.

Tony Massengill

Guru Dan Inosanto once told me that "teaching is the highest form of learning." As a martial arts educator, I have utilized reflective teaching and learning to continuously enhance my Wing Chun practice.

William Kwok

You must also be careful of student/teacher relationships. In my experience, jealousy can unfortunately play a part in driving a rift between student and teacher. At some point, every bird must leave the nest, but it would be nice to pick a teacher who won't push you out and then try to eat you.

Randy Williams

To apply Wing Chun and fight, the forms chi sao and muk yan chong are not enough. These are just the basics to help you understand the ideas of Wing Chun. Nobody fights in the form.

Alan Lee

In the Western world there are styles that emphasize the ground-fighting aspect of the style and others that have implemented a number of concepts they took from weapons programs. There are fantastic and not so fantastic schools in both the East and the West.

Thommy L. Boehlig

PHILOSOPHY

When people label any martial art as a sport, they probably only see the superficial appearance of it. You might discover some martial arts applications concealed within any style.

Carson Lau

Consistency of hard work training will guarantee results. Intensity often brings failure. Be aware of your talents; it's a good thing but could easily bring laziness.

Lin Xiang Fuk

If a Wing Chun practitioner only learns the fighting techniques or sparring, that person's Wing Chun skill may only be able to reach a certain level.

Gorden Lu

Wing Chun is like a treasure. I am so lucky my sifus have shared their knowledge with me; through them and through training in Wing Chun.

Alan Lee

When you talk about fighting, your eyes, your ears, your nose are not as important as your sense of touch. You could say that chi sao is a very limited kind of sparring, as opposed to free sparring, which would be unlimited.

Jim Lau

Once people start to see the effectiveness of Wing Chun, the market will grow. Wing Chun is an advanced art that continues to grow with the practitioner.

Gary Lam

I believe that one of my greatest values as a teacher is that I have no political agenda, nor do I have any affiliation with any of the big wing chun groups who are promoting themselves throughout the U.S.

Alan Lamb

The kind of power used in Wing Tsun does not come from big muscles and that big muscles actually prevent the kind of "energy" and "power" that a good Wing Tsun punch must possess.

Leung Ting

You might have a better fighting theory behind your system, but if your skill level is lower than your opponent's skill, you'll be easily defeated. All the theory in the world can't save you from losing.

Wong Shun Leung

I just plan to train and teach the best Wing Chun I am capable of. I plan to continue my training and research in the art.

Tony Massengill

I want all my students to have their own Wing Chun style. They should not fight like me. They should fight like them but with a base on Wing Chun principles.

Gorden Lu

When I started, there were very few teachers. I think the standard of teaching has fallen; hence, that is why I continue teaching. My goal is to pass on the traditional Ip Man Family Wing Chun Style.

Samuel Kwok

A Sifu such as myself, who reinvents Wing Tsun each day, and who builds everything on the principles and explains everything by them, must be more of a curse than a blessing for some.

Keith R. Kernspecht

Today people take up martial arts as a past-time, for health reasons, exercise, to impress their friends or for self-defense, but they don't seem to want to spend too much time and effort on it. This means that the modern instructtors have to please them as a customer, not as a student.

Victor Kan

You need to realize that Wing Chun is like mathematics: you can improve or expand the formula, but you can't change the fact that one plus one equals two.

Jim Fung

I tell my students that the most important thing is to keep an open mind. Keep learning and keep growing. Keep giving and sharing your knowledge with others.

Francis Fong

You can mix styles, but I recommend focusing on one style in the beginning. Otherwise, you can simply get a superficial knowledge of the art and never understand it fully to reach higher levels of development.

Augustine Fong

Research well before choosing an instructor to learn from. Be patient in training, don't try to rush the learning process. Work and train hard, be diligent in their studies.

Ip Chun

To become proficient in the Wing Chun style, several important qualities are necessary. I heavily emphasize not only teaching my students the physical techniques but also the philosophical aspects of Chinese tradition and martial virtues.

William Kwok

There is no doubt that supplementary training improves your conditioning. Just remember—a good runner can't fight, but a good fighter can run. A weightlifter can't fight, but a good fighter can lift.

Chung Kwok Chow

I am a big advocate of cross-training, but I believe you have to have a strong root and basis in one system you identify with. I firmly believe that you win with your basics and what you trained in the most. Not try to be a "jack-of-all-trades," simply because you've studied a bit in all of them.

Robert Chu

I teach my students with an emphasis on self-defense using a hybrid of modern and traditional methods. Some people are fascinated by history and tradition, but I think self-defense should be the main focus of martial arts.

Carson Lau

Wing Chun is a very good method for someone interested in realistic Martial skills. Just train hard and gain an understanding of the principles of the art.

Ip Ching

The discipline in martial arts comes from respect and integrity. Unfortunately, some people seem to have forgotten what those are all about.

William Cheung

Physical and strong tool development is more important than the techniques. The way you apply techniques comes from your courage or confidence. You gain courage and confidence through your experience.

Hawkins Cheung

My philosophy with regards to my own training is simple—keep an open mind, always seek knowledge, and never assume that you know everything.

David Peterson

By combining tradition and modernity, we can keep the martial arts alive and relevant. We have the opportunity to showcase the beauty and effectiveness of Wing Tsun while meeting the needs and demands of today. By instilling discipline, respect and perseverance in our students, we can help them grow not only as martial artists, but also as people of integrity and self-confidence.

Mohammed Ince

I found there are some similarities between Wing Chun and other Martial Arts. Of course, there are differences in terms of techniques but the overall objective in attack and defense is the same.

Au Yeung

There are a lot of masters out there with great personalities and a tremendous understanding and experience in the styles they teach. They have reached levels of skill that others can only dream of.

Emin Boztepe

I follow my Sifu's way, which is quality, not quantity and having a full-time job means my 40 year passion remains just that and I can be selective who I teach and remain true to what I was taught.

Shaun Rawcliffe

Through the many drills inherent in the system, such as "Paak Sau," "Laap Sau" and of course "Chi Sau" (in its many variants), we then develop the means to "communicate" with our opponent in a language of combat that is simple, direct and efficient.

David Peterson

Personally, I grew up in a family where I didn't have to fight much and since I always looked up to "tough guys" as a teenager, this testosterone driven scene gave me enough "role models" to find my own place in the martial arts world.

Thommy L. Boehlig

I personally don't look at the Martial Arts from a philosophical direction. I am Christian, so the Eastern religious background and philosophy hold no interest for me. I train the Martial Arts strictly from a practical application point of view.

Tony Massengill

My own view of what is important in wing chun can at times be very different from many other traditional kung-fu instructors.

Randy Williams

I personally don't believe in mixing Kung Fu styles. I am of the Traditional Progressive Mindset. It really depends on what is your goal.

Lin Xiang Fuk

People who want to learn Wing Chun only need to focus on three things: First, understand the basic Wing Chun theories; second, learn how to react with your natural reaction; and third, relax and enjoy.

Gorden Lu

In Wing Chun like in any other style martial art, too many people want to be the chief and nobody wants to be an Indian. I'm still an Indian.

Jim Lau

Many school owners in Europe are very protective of their curriculum and students and there is a sense of mistrust and competition that I have come across a number of times in the past.

Thommy L. Boehlig

I want serious students only. I tell people interested in learning Wing Chun to look at other schools first to make sure they see what's available and not commit to something without doing more research.

Alan Lee

Wing Chun is the most advanced, direct, and scientific art that has been proven to work in real situations.

Gary Lam

It is also important to acknowledge that traditional martial arts have their own value systems that prioritize principles such as martial virtues and self-defense skills in real-life situations.

William Kwok

I truly believe that wing chun is the best self defense art that a woman can study and use effectively.

Alan Lamb

Unfortunately, age inevitably diminishes our physical capabilities. Therefore, when you are young use your body to train your mind and when you get older… use your mind to train your body.

Leung Ting

PHILOSOPHY

When you are young you like to fight. As you grow, you look at fighting in a different way. You have a different point of view about physical confrontations. It is important to educate the students about this.

Wong Shun Leung

The Wing Chun practitioner always should aim to control the other person's two hands with only one of his/her own hands. This creates the situation in which it is very difficult (if not near impossible) to be counterattacked.

Samuel Kwok

As Bruce Lee rightly said, "They all only do something that is 'vaguely related' to self-defense."

Keith R. Kernspecht

There are many modified versions of Wing Chun in the world nowadays. Those instructors go around saying that "in the 21st century, everything needs to be modified."

Victor Kan

All instructors must be willing to put aside their egos to seek further instruction from genuine Wing Chun masters or grandmasters to improve their knowledge and skills further. This will no doubt help the Wing Chun art to perpetuate.

Jim Fung

My love for the arts came naturally to me. I was very passionate about Wing Chun, so practicing was never a chore.

Francis Fong

The non-classical concept can be fully realized only after years of practicing the fundamentals. At this level, the fighter becomes more independent, developing his own fighting style, and his own ideas. It becomes the "master" of the art and its principles. The practitioner *is* the style.

Augustine Fong

I respect all methods and believe they all have some benefit, but my personal studies have been limited to Wing Chun. I am not sure if studying several systems of martial arts is something positive or negative.

Ip Chun

PHILOSOPHY

We know there is no one style that covers all four ranges in fighting (long range, close range, takedown range, and ground range). Mixing other kung fu styles with yours helps you to understand about different situations of fighting. It is the positive thing to do.

Chung Kwok Chow

The Siu Lim Tao and Chum Kiu share one pizza slice because they make use of the opponent's force in the same way: both softly absorb incoming force and direct it away from the practitioner's body. Defensive techniques are relatively soft and the practitioner seeks to feel the opponent's intention early and to slow his attacks down by softly absorbing his attacks.

Thommy L. Boehlig

In martial arts, natural athletes rarely last. The martial arts are an acquired skill; they have to be learned. Some people learn things quickly and just burn out quickly.

Robert Chu

Wing Chun is a very good method for someone interested in realistic Martial skills. Just train hard and gain an understanding of the principles of the art.

Ip Ching

Wing chun specializes in close-quarter combat. I teach three stages of combat: the pre-contact stage, the contact stage, and the pursuit and retreat stage.

William Cheung

Don't fight it if you have too much to lose. If you must fight, you must destroy your opponent and not stop until he is defeated.

Hawkins Cheung

Always challenge what you already know and always ask yourself how you can do it better.

Au Yeung

Every student or instructor, after immersing themselves in martial arts for a long period of time, will experience different stages of realization and understanding.

Kim Man Chan

Later on, I became interested in the philosophical side of the martial arts and I began reading books on the topic, thus allowing me to search for and bring forward the sensitive side of my personality.

Emin Boztepe

Biu Tze is kind of set apart. If your training, deployment and utilization of Siu Nim Tao and Chum Kiu was perfect, then you would never need Biu Tze, since Biu Tze, (also known as "Gow Gup Sao"— emergency hand) is to recover from mistakes.

Shaun Rawcliffe

Be patient, progress will show through consistent training. Remember there are no secret techniques, techniques are special only after you put your hard work in practicing it.

Carson Lau

Either train your students in a fashion that prepares them for real combat, getting them to face the reality of what that entails, both physically and emotionally, or be honest and tell them that you are merely practicing a sport which does not guarantee any real fighting ability.

David Peterson

I have always been pretty good at learning physical movement. The most difficult thing in Wing Chun was the concept of relaxation during the act of defending against attack. I found Chi Sao training to be a great method of developing this attribute.

Tony Massengill

I believe that both combat sports and traditional martial arts have their respective benefits, and it is up to individuals to determine which practice aligns with their goals and values.

William Kwok

I believe that martial arts will always move forward with the times, as they must. As in all other forms of science and technology, I believe that wing chun and martial arts in general must move ahead, adapting and improving to keep pace with the rest of the world.

Randy Williams

During my early years, my training was very painful as none of my Kung Fu brothers had any mercy, especially the one who was the most senior.

Lin Xiang Fuk

Wing chun is truly based on yin and yang. It is the perfect balance between two opposing forces.

Alan Lamb

Wing Chun is very abstract. We learn to fight from the theories. Other styles may emphasize hard power, but Wing Chun can be hard or soft depending on the opponent and situation.

Gorden Lu

I personally don't see the need to train more than one style as Wing Chun encourages the practitioner to take the simple tools and explore their own applications.

Shaun Rawcliffe

Ving Tsun goal is the quick and total incapacitation of the enemy, reversing the roles of attacker and victim within the first one or two blows being thrown.

David Peterson

The movements in the forms by themselves are not used in fighting, but you can combine them or use them a little differently than the way they are practiced in the form to create a technique to encounter a situation.

Alan Lee

Competence at self-defense is only partly a product of chi sao practice. Also necessary for development of real fighting ability is training in footwork, free sparring, and in strategy or tactics.

Jim Lau

Besides his fighting and Wing Chun skills, my Sifu Wong Shun Leung also was very open, kind- hearted, and had a great sense of humor.

Gary Lam

Wing Tsun is based on reaction and how to use a certain training to efficiently protect yourself from any kind of attack.

Leung Ting

I can only say that I try to share wing chun in an honest way. I teach in a logical manner because the art is very logical.

Wong Shun Leung

I think it is important to have an open mind when it comes to your quest for knowledge of martial arts.

Samuel Kwok

The conventional Wing Tsun (Wing Chun, Ving Tsun) is something external, or in the best case something half external and half internal.

Keith R. Kernspecht

Kung Fu means time and energy expended on work. We can use Kung Fu as an adjective to describe the ability of a professional man.

Victor Kan

To me, kung fu is a holistic practice that involves physical, mental, and spiritual development. While there is a competitive aspect to kung fu, the ultimate goal is not just to win competitions but also to cultivate oneself and become a better person.

William Kwok

Irrespective of the effectiveness of the style, all Martial Arts are beneficial and unique in their own way. Hence, students or followers do their best to preserve their own styles.

Jim Fung

I always understood Kung Fu to mean "achievement through great effort," or simply "virtue." Originally, to practice "kung fu" did not just mean to practice Chinese martial arts.

Francis Fong

Timing is a very tricky part of the Wing Chun system. There are many different types of timing, and you need to know when to use them. Timing is really the foundation of speed. If the timing is right, the speed is right.

Augustine Fong

The learning in Wing Chun never ends. Your knowledge in the art depends on how much research you do to understand the application of the style to different situations and fighting methods.

Alan Lee

I have had many Western students over the years who have become very good teachers of Wing Chun and are now passing the system to their own students. This brings me a great deal of happiness.

Ip Chun

Most kung fu styles focus on long range, while Wing Chun focuses on close range. Some of them focus on showmanship, while Wing Chun focuses on practicality. In general, most kung fu styles focus on power and speed, while Wing Chun focuses on sensitivity for leverage and timing.

Chung Kwok Chow

I try to use the sports theories in developing the supporting exercises to give my students an advantage in learning Wing Chun in the shortest period of time to reach the same high quality.

Gorden Lu

The system is based on the most effective use of human body and proper timing and positioning. Everything is dependent upon the moment and the energy that the opponent gives us.

Robert Chu

The student has to find a good instructor who not only understands the system but is concerned with passing that knowledge to their student.

Ip Ching

Bruce Lee always looked on me as a role model in wing chun. This can be a problem because you don't let your own potential come out naturally. You're always thinking about somebody else.

William Cheung

If a drunk driver is driving a Ferrari and crashes the car into a tree, it is obviously the driver and not the car that is at fault. The situation is similar in martial arts. Success depends on individual skill, training, and personal dedication, not solely on the martial art itself.

Mohammed Ince

Personally, I don't like titles such as master or grandmaster.

Thommy L. Boehlig

Offense is based on attack; defense is based on body structure. Offense is only 50 percent of the art. Many Wing Chun men only concentrate on the offensive portion because offense is the best defense.

Hawkins Cheung

I don't think you can ever reach a level and stop and be done with it. It is not constant, and I will always be involved in some sort of training every day. I see constantly improving myself as a lifetime development. Never give up and always improve on what you already have.

Au Yeung

If you go into the martial arts, you deal with your fears and your complexes right away. There's no escape. It's hands on. You're forced to use your brain differently; you're forced to open up yourself and you're forced to learn how to deal with your own problems.

Emin Boztepe

I don't teach for a living so I am in the privileged position where I can be very selective whom I teach; every potential student has to go through a 16-lesson probationary period so I can judge their character, dedication and suitability for Wing Chun.

Shaun Rawcliffe

I think that some instructors water down the reality side of training in order to retain students and keep people happy.

David Peterson

My personal Wing Chun is a synthesis of all I have learned from all of the instructors I have had over the years. I believe that Wing Chun is a living art. Not fixed, not stagnant, but continually developing

Tony Massengill

Kung Fu Is a way of unifying mind, body, and spirit. A way of building strength, confidence, and lifelong relationships.

Randy Williams

Everybody can train as hard as they want, to progress their skill as high as they possibly can. It's a lifelong journey.

Lin Xiang Fuk

Everybody who learns Wing Chun has a purpose, condition, talent, and background and they may always focus on something more than another.

Gorden Lu

A sifu should not think he is too smart and invent his own way to play the form and the techniques. Doing this will misguide students from correctly understanding Wing Chun's basic ideas and will water down the style's effectiveness.

Alan Lee

Wing chun is constantly hitting, and where there is an empty gap, you hit. The saying in wing chun is, "When the hand slips off, straight lunge."

Jim Lau

As long as I remain curious and continue to ask questions, there will always be something new to discover in the world of Wing Chun.

William Kwok

I think that American students in general put more emphasis on creativity, Chinese students on traditional values, and the Europeans on discipline.

Gary Lam

I would say, in general, students should be wary of people who claim to be masters of every style. It's not possible! Avoid the "jack of all trades" approach to the martial arts.

Alan Lamb

Your ability to use the Wing Tsun techniques will depend entirely on you and how you can actually use these in a practical application under various real circumstances.

Leung Ting

Wing chun theory is flawless if you can execute it perfectly. But a theory is just a theory. It means nothing if you can't put it to work.

Wong Shun Leung

I have no special talents and had to work as hard as anybody to develop my skills. In fact, even after all these years, I am still working on them—the journey doesn't end until we die!

David Peterson

Each style has its own specialty and method of dealing with opponents. So, if a full-contact tournament has rules or restrictions prohibiting certain types of attacks, inevitably some styles will be disadvantaged.

Alan Lee

All three Wing Chun forms are related to each other but have their own meaning and purpose. The Siu Lim Tao form teaches you all the basic techniques that are then used in combination in Chum Kiu and Biu Jee. The three forms all are to prepare us for Chi Sao, which prepares us for fighting.

Samuel Kwok

If Ng Mui and Yim Wing Tsun had studied sports and movement science with Prof. Tiwald, they would have put the horse before the cart!

Keith R. Kernspecht

My students learn other martial art systems in addition to Wing Chun, to become well-rounded. In my opinion, I believe that the more you learn, the more well-rounded you are.

Francis Fong

In Wing Chun, your basic structure is composed of your stance, your bong sau, tan sau, and fook sau. These have to be really strong to prevent the body being knocked off balance when in contact with an opponent's arms in combat.

Jim Fung

I did meet the Grandmaster Yip Man although I never trained with him. Yip Man didn't believe in teaching kids, women or poor people. He thought that you had to work hard to make a decent living first, and then study Wing Chun.

Augustine Fong

Integrity, respect, and good character. Kung Fu must follow the path of virtue. A Kung Fu man without virtue is dangerous to his fellow man.

Ip Chun

Wing Chun was invented by a woman (probably the only martial art invented by a woman) who solved problems by maximizing her power, speed, and sensitivity. My most important points of teaching are based on "Wing Chun's Eight Theories."

Chung Kwok Chow

I hope martial artists can study the martial arts to avoid delusion, stupidity, greed, envy, anger and hatred. It's a good medium to develop friendship and understand more about life.

Robert Chu

I encourage students to get out of the Wing Chun system and come back so they know the others.

William Cheung

Some westerners do well but many do not have the patience to train in a traditional sense. Too many are more interested in having a title (Master, Sifu) rather than developing the knowledge and skill necessary to earn those titles.

Ip Ching

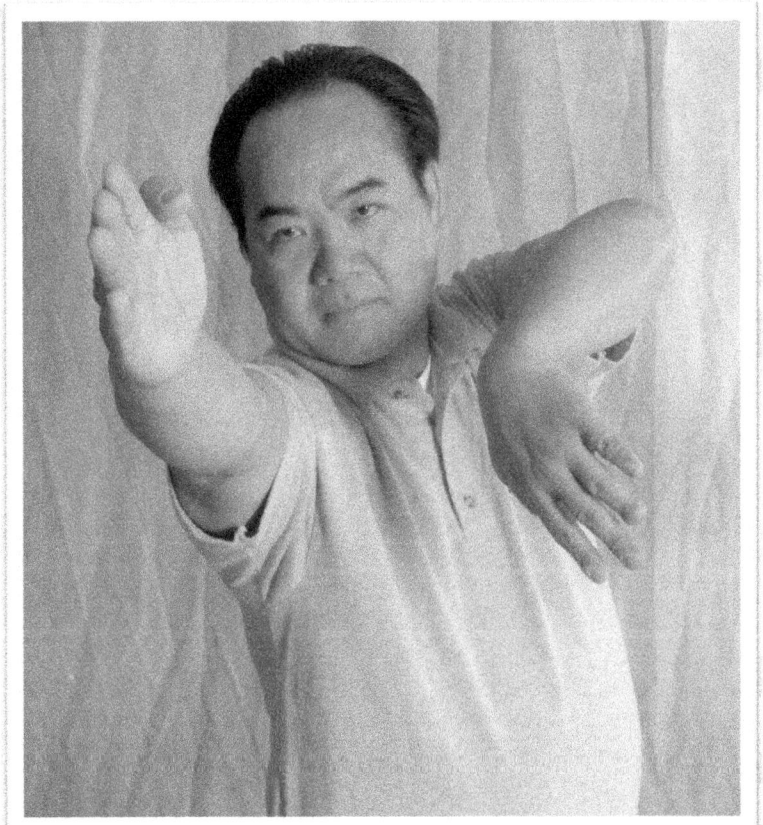

The most important weapon in Wing Chun is the mind. The mind is the center, the "referee" that the system revolves around. Having a calm mind will determine your success in combat. The Wing Chun mind is the mental frame of mind you need to survive.

Hawkins Cheung

My students and my family give me the motivation to get up every day. I also want to make my family proud, knowing that I am able to pursue my passion, teaching and spreading the art of Wing Tsun Kung Fu.

Carson Lau

I think the Westerners' approach to Martial Arts is more focused on the result and efficiency but a Chinese kung fu practitioner is more focused internally—the psychological effect and health of body and mind.

Au Yeung

One day the art becomes part of your life and is a way of expressing yourself and do something that you love in this world. For me martial arts are a way of life, they are my life.

Emin Boztepe

Every student is potentially one of the next generation of instructors, so it is important to get the right personalities.

Shaun Rawcliffe

Teaching the art of kung fu is a multifaceted practice about self-improvement that encompasses self-defense, health, and tradition. While all of these elements are important, I believe that self-defense should be the top priority.

William Kwok

For me personally, the meaning of the practice of Kung Fu is self-fulfillment. It has enabled me to improve who I am and to give something of value to others through teaching the system and writing about it.

David Peterson

I consider myself a perpetual student. If I am not studying, learning, and researching how to be better, I am not happy.

Tony Massengill

Each person is different and must strive to find the things that make them stronger spiritually. Some people find it in religion, others in charity work. But whatever it is that you need to do to make yourself feel "clean" and "deserving" will also serve to strengthen your spirit.

Randy Williams

Real Kung Fu means real hard work. No hard work means not real Kung Fu.

Lin Xiang Fuk

No ultimate martial art exists that is the best choice for everyone. Each person brings different physical conditions, interests, and goals. Therefore, it makes sense to choose the fighting style that best suits you and supports your personal goals.

Mohammed Ince

From my point of view, Wing Chun is like any other Martial Arts style; they all have something special and unique.

Gorden Lu

Only once the basic techniques, functions, positions, and associated energies have been developed and understood through the forms and associated drills, is it possible to apply freely, explore, and react according to the fluid and unpredictable scenarios, responses and techniques faced within Chi Sao.

Shaun Rawcliffe

I have found little difference between Easterners and Westerners when it comes to training. Right at the beginning, all find the serious training to be torturous, tiring, and painful.

Alan Lee

Interestingly, in many respects, the long pole is even closer in nature to the concepts/ actions of the empty-hand component of the system than the knife form is, which is one of the reasons why it is usually taught earlier than the knife form.

David Peterson

During the practice of chi sao a person is gradually getting used to the feel of the range. When you fight you have to get in close - if you can't touch, you can't hit.

Jim Lau

I only like to teach what works in the real world, and the students need to understand the logic behind every move.

Gary Lam

Wing Chun can be learned by any- body, respective of age because you don't have to be super flexible or particularly acrobatic to do it.

Alan Lamb

Biu Jee introduces us to what can be called "emergency" tools showing the student a series of technical resources extremely important in practical self-defense circumstances.

Leung Ting

I think the wing chun method is ugly for movies but very good and very logical for real fighting.

Wong Shun Leung

Those who want to learn quickly are going away with a framework but have nothing inside the framework (it's like the skin on an orange: it can look good but how good can it be if the inside is not as good as the outside looks).

Samuel Kwok

Relax, yet be pressure loaded! Relax in your training, relax your interactions with others and relax in the way you treat yourself. But maintain that hunger, that forward flow and willingness to accomplish something.

Thommy L. Boehlig

Normally, you don't do Chi Sao until you have learned Sil Lum Tao because you need to have good stability and a strong structure, bong sau and fook sau.

Jim Fung

Wing Chun really is simple, but it's not easy. Also, you need to have more patience and discipline. Not many people are willing to put the time into it, especially beginners.

Francis Fong

In Wing Chun there really isn't a direct relationship between the way you do the forms and how you apply the movements in Chi Sao. The real application of the moves found in the forms will be determined by the opponent and the amount of force and type energy he gives you.

Augustine Fong

PHILOSOPHY

I believe the health benefits of Kung Fu are just as important as the martial aspects. From the beginning I enjoyed Kung Fu but have concentrated more on health than fighting. I never looked for fights and I think the true spirit of the Martial Arts is to avoid fights not to star.

Ip Chun

I think styles are important since they represent kung fu's skills and history. There are so many ways in fighting. Some are good in long range, so they are best using longer limbs. Some are good in close range, so they strike with shorter limbs. There is no one style that has the best of all ranges. I try very hard to train in all ranges because I recognize the value they contribute.

Chung Kwok Chow

Only through application can you prove if the theories are valid. Techniques without timing are dead techniques.

Hawkins Cheung

Everything is dependent upon the moment and the energy that the opponent gives us. People are not entirely correct when they think that wing chun is only scientific and based on physics—the basics are the science but the expression in application is the art.

Robert Chu

Too many students neglect their training time. Without proper dedication to training, people cannot progress and develop the skill of Wing Chun.

Ip Ching

Master Yip told me to take care of Bruce because we were always involved in fights, and I was his senior. I had the responsibility of leading him a little bit.

William Cheung

Politics may seem to be fun at first sight and in the beginning of a situation but after a while only bring the art and the teachers of the art together with the students down the drain.

Emin Boztepe

My Martial Art has matured and developed immensely, and my reason for training has also changed totally. I initially started Martial Arts as I was bullied at school and needed to build my self-confidence.

Shaun Rawcliffe

Systems have specific concepts or techniques that they use to attain their combat goals. If you try to combine such concepts or techniques with methods that are completely different, I cannot see much benefit being achieved.

David Peterson

My teaching methods focus on the practical application o f Wing Chun in a violent street environment. Too many Martial Arts suffer from what I call "sport leakage" in their training.

Tony Massengill

In your training, try to keep mind, body, and spirit in balance. It is easy to train the body with forms, drills, sparring, weight training, et cetera but the mind is a little harder to train.

Randy Williams

The important qualities for students to become proficient are a willingness to empty their cup (have an open mind), hard work, ego control, character/behavior and compassion.

Lin Xiang Fuk

The Wing Chun system just pro- vides this training, so people who learn Wing Chun may not need to spend a lot of time then they can easier hands on and apply to situation.

Gorden Lu

It is not until the student has had an actual fighting experience that he can understand why traditional training is so important, because the training teaches you how to respond to an attacker.

Alan Lee

Other than training hard, having patience, and maintaining a strong interest, the most important quality for a student to become proficient in Wing Chun is "understanding."

Gary Lam

One of the most important things for practitioners is to cultivate grit, which means having the power of passion and perseverance. This involves sticking with your training even during tough times and continuously pushing yourself to improve over time.

William Kwok

I feel obliged to pass on my knowledge and skills to others. Seeing how the student develops is my biggest motivation. I feel responsible for ensuring that the knowledge and techniques of martial arts are not lost and want to ensure that the next generation of martial artists can carry them forward.

Mohammed Ince

If the forms are the textbooks of wing chun, then chi sao is probably best described as a "living laboratory." Within the laboratory, practitioners of this style of kung-fu may experiment and analyze all the technical movements previously learned.

Jim Lau

I do not encourage my students or anyone to participate in street fights. Street fights are very dangerous, and anything can happen.

Carson Lau

I want to open up people's minds to the value of wing chun. I really feel that it has a lot to offer people of all ages.

Alan Lamb

PHILOSOPHY

Wing Chun is not really fancy. You have to work on coordination and emphasize energy. So, it is not easy for Westerners to accept, because they don't grow up with the same cultural approach.

Francis Fong

You should always avoid the fight. Do not look for it and try to avoid it at all costs. This is what I teach to my students.

Leung Ting

In Wing Chun everything comes naturally through Chi Sao training. Since there are almost no prearranged combinations in Chi Sao, the student applies the techniques as he or she pleases. This teaches him to react spontaneously—whether training at the "kwoon' or on the street.

Augustine Fong

Basically, I teach the same method I learned from Yip Man, but I would say that I teach it in a more systematic way. At the same time, though, I'm still very intuitive in my teaching.

Wong Shun Leung

You need to get the students to use their brains to find out why a technique works, to understand the principles and theories, to understand the "keys." It is 50 percent from the sifu and 50 percent from the student.

Samuel Kwok

Wing Chun does not involve any kicks above waist height. Kicks this high can be caught by an opponent and higher kicks cause the exponent to lose power.

Jim Fung

We see the plant growing, if we begin pulling on it, in order to help it grow, we will only kill it. The same is true of Kung Fu. It takes time for skill to develop. We simply cannot rush the process. We must let the natural learning process take place.

Ip Chun

I am always looking for better ways and setting higher goals. I believe Wing Chun has one of the best theories, so it deserves to be expanded to other fighting ranges, especially the ground range, which I call "chi-sun," which means "sticky body."

Chung Kwok Chow

You cannot fight if you are not in good health.

Ip Ching

You study martial arts for you—not for what names you can drop. All those names and credentials don't help when you're being attacked.

Robert Chu

Bruce Lee realized that if you're not in shape then you're out of business in martial arts.

William Cheung

A Wing Chun player captures the centerline first, which means he has the opponent targeted. If I am pointing my gun at you, and you move, even slightly, I'll shoot.

Hawkins Cheung

Another critical element of successful training is keeping an open mind. This means being willing to learn from others and try new things, even if they do not fit into your existing worldview or training style.

William Kwok

Wing Chun gives you focus and perspective of things. In the end, martial arts are something you do for yourself, it's something you can take with you no matter where you go, no matter what your environment may be.

Emin Boztepe

I think there is a martial art out there to suit everyone, some styles which are very athletic and require a great deal of flexibility, others are hard and physically punishing.

Shaun Rawcliffe

Mixing styles is not guaranteed to produce better results—in fact, it may end up decreasing one's ability to fight well at all.

David Peterson

We have an old saying in law enforcement that "We don't rise to the occasion; we sink to our level of training." The meaning is that we react according to the way we train.

Tony Massengill

If the teacher needs work on his stop-kick skills, it would be better for him to focus on that aspect in his own personal regimen, rather than use to large a portion of valuable class time that would be better spent on those things needed by a group that's not ready for such things.

Randy Williams

Kung Fu is an art that has many different varieties. It's important to find out what fits you best. The style is the person.

Lin Xiang Fuk

In Wing Chun, we don't learn how to hit. We learn how to not get hit. We always cover our opening and make sure we are safe and control the situation then hit back.

Gorden Lu

The movements of Wing Chun were designed to fit the human body's natural movements, and all of the art's ideas and movements can be explained in a scientific way.

Alan Lee

I assess students by the quality of their output not the quantity of their input. My students are taught to assess their own abilities in the same manner.

Jim Lau

Students also need to set realistic goals. Bruce Lee did not become the best fighter overnight.

Gary Lam

I would like to see more women studying wing chun, especially in view of the recent increase in violent crimes against women, especially sexual assault. I think women definitely need to learn something.

Alan Lamb

It is important that as true martial artists we strive to stay away from any physical confrontation that involves hurting any other human being.

Leung Ting

While jeet kune do was a significant art for Bruce, it has not been that way for other people who followed his method.

Wong Shun Leung

I tell my students that it is always good to observe other styles of martial arts, so that you can see the techniques and think how you will be able to "feel" these techniques.

Samuel Kwok

The moment you think you achieve the top level, that's the time you stop progressing. I don't want to stop at any point.

Lin Xiang Fuk

Most fights start close in after an argument and Wing Chun trains for close combat. We use fast, low kicks and powerful punches delivered from a short distance.

Jim Fung

Wing Chun is the foundation and tool to help me to discover my own potential. Learning Wing Chun helped me to recognize body mechanics and structure, which I then adapted into different martial arts.

Francis Fong

PHILOSOPHY

There is nothing wrong with sport Kung Fu. People just need to understand that there is a difference between sport and Martial art. In sport, there are limitations and rules. This is not true of a real self-defense encounter.

Ip Chun

Try to stick closely to the Wooden Dummy because this will develop economy of technique. Also, try to flow from one complete motion to another and not stopping between motions because this will disrupt the flow and retards the development of body mechanics.

Augustine Fong

Avoid three things: greed, anger, and stupidity. Don't ever think you're a master or a Buddha. You have to always be a student of life.

Robert Chu

In Wing Chun, we train to develop conditioned reflex. If those conditioned reflexes are based on a sport with limiting rules, you may not respond as you need to in a real situation.

Ip Ching

In my Wing Chun concept, I like the opponent to start first. I will initiate my timing from my opponent's start. To my experience, this movement is a trap.

Hawkins Cheung

I believe fear is the key that help the individual to find a lot of answers about himself—and I'm not strictly speaking about martial arts. Fear is your "blood brother"—it's always there, no matter where you go, and the tricky part is that there are many reasons why the fear appears in our lives.

Emin Boztepe

I don't believe Wing Chun has any place in Full Contact tournaments. I do respect and admire anyone who has the confidence to enter such competitions, however, I learnt Wing Chun for simple, practical self defence... no rules, no referees, no corner-man, no protection, no tap- ping out and no instant medical treatment available.

Shaun Rawcliffe

I think that it is necessary to train with regularity and to drill skills under pressure as often as possible. I'm not so sure that sparring is the best way to go because it does tend to become a game of "tit-for-tat" if not monitored well.

David Peterson

I believe that if one is teaching what they are calling "Ip Man Wing Chun," it should be in line with the structural foundation that Ip Man taught.

Tony Massengill

I constantly review all of my old notes from years gone by and I never fail to pick up on some concept, technique, or drill that I hadn't thought of for decades.

Randy Williams

Wing Chun has already been popular for years and many people are still interested in it for its emphasis on traditional training, not "fast-food Kung Fu."

Gorden Lu

Innovation implies "new" and if one seriously studies the past he will find that we are generally rediscovering our potential.

Jim Lau

The reason for the change in the teaching methodology is that the student-teacher relationship is so different now. The student-teacher relationship used to be like a father-son relationship. But now the student is more like a customer the teacher has to please.

Alan Lee

Wing Chun is based on directness, logic, and centerline.

Gary Lam

In Kung Fu training, this philosophy is reflected in the emphasis on cultivating virtues such as discipline, perseverance, humility, and respect for others. The physical practice of Kung Fu is also seen as a means of developing the mind and spirit, as well as the body. Techniques such as meditation and Qi Gong are often incorporated into training to cultivate inner strength, focus, and mindfulness.

Mohammed Ince

Sifu Wong taught me many aspects of chin-na, self-defense techniques, and weapons. However, before he would consent to teach me, he looked deeply into my eyes to read what kind of person I was.

Alan Lamb

We only need to fight when we are truly in danger in a situation where any other solution is not possible.

Leung Ting

I believe most Westerners generally place a lot more emphasis on the fitness aspect while most traditional Chinese kung fu practitioners treat it more as an art.

Jim Fung

In the later days of his life Bruce said to me, "If I could take back jeet kune do, I'd take it back." He realized that he could make the movements work, but that was because his style was designed for his own specific talents.

Wong Shun Leung

I encourage all my students to analyze what they have learned from me, reflect upon their analyses, and return to the next training session with a list of questions that will enhance their understanding.

Samuel Kwok

As teachers we have to simulate realistic situations and then gradually make them more and more real so that the student doesn't feel like a fish out of water if he should ever have a real-life encounter.

Thommy L. Boehlig

Wing Chun is all about self-development. I always learn and my students give me that opportunity. I learn from my associates, my friends, my students—everybody. Without them, I would never grow.

Francis Fong

There is a reason for every detail in Wing Chun. I want my students to understand why we do each technique, why certain positions and movements work better and how to correct and improve themselves.

Alan Lee

Kung fu means to cultivate. Every day cultivate a little and improve a little. Soon all will be clear.

Robert Chu

PHILOSOPHY

It is important to understand that all of the Wing Chun forms contain principles that can be used at varying distances. For example, Biu Jee's emergency techniques can be combined with Siu Lim Tau principles to deal with situations involving greater distance and time.

Augustine Fong

Wing Chun is based on efficiency. There is no wasted motion. Wing Chun is simply about being efficient in a real fight.

Ip Ching

One of the big problems with Wing Chun as spread in the West, is instructors teaching incomplete or made-up Wing Chun, due to instructors establishing classes, who never completed training in the system. This has been a problem in the West.

Ip Chun

Change and adaptation are essential to survival. That is why there are so many types of martial arts. He insisted that like an immigrant, you have to change your ways to adapt to your new environment A good Wing Chun player is a great pretender. He can adapt and change his tactics. You must change and adapt to circumstances to survive!

Hawkins Cheung

My motivation for learning Wing Chun has only grown stronger over the years. The complexity of this martial art means that there is always more to discover, which is what excites me and keeps me motivated.

William Kwok

Let me put it this way; I don't like to fight. I don't look for people and start fights. It's not my personality. I'm a martial art teacher than can fight. I don't talk bad about anyone but if someone talks bad about me then I'll confront him.

Emin Boztepe

In the street you aren't trained to peak fitness for a fight you knew of months in advance; you aren't facing an opponent who is known to you.

Shaun Rawcliffe

If you are not hitting something often, or working out with training partners often, then you are at the wrong school. Wing Chun is about interaction and about real combat skills—you don't get that from standing in the line throwing punches all the time.

David Peterson

If one is going to teach things they have developed, they need to be ethical enough to be honest about that fact and let it stand on its own merit. It is wrong to attempt to get undue credibility by a false claim that it was taught by Ip Man.

Tony Massengill

I think it would be better to say that sport is only a small facet of the full spectrum of meaning covered by the term "martial arts."

Randy Williams

As a teacher, we must bear the responsibility to pass the system as it is without holding anything back to ensure the preservation to future generation.

Lin Xiang Fuk

As a Wing Chun Sifu I am not just teaching, I also learn from teaching. I have found similarities between teaching Wing Chun and my police job. There is always something new every day.

Gorden Lu

Without truly comprehensive study, which entails far more than casual study of a multitude of styles over a period of years, the non-traditionalist goal of attaining sophisticated analytical abilities is simply a myth.

Jim Lau

Regardless of style, I believe all schools should have a refined curriculum that teaches students to understand the ideas and theories behind their techniques, analyze what is correct, improve their techniques, and make their techniques more efficient.

Alan Lee

My biggest inspiration is seeing my students grow. I love teaching them and I see myself in them. Their growth reflects my own.

Carson Lau

The long pole helps the coordination of hand, leg, and body, sitting power, movements, and accuracy, while the butterfly knives teach us to change under different conditions.

Gary Lam

When facing a knife or a gun the best solution is to run. Don't try to be a hero.

Leung Ting

I have always liked boxing-I like anything about fighting, but my kind of fighting is not the sport version, it is real fighting where there are no rules, no restrictions, and your life is hanging in the balance.

Wong Shun Leung

I want the art (Ip Man Family Wing Chun Kung Fu System) to flourish and be passed on the correct way of the Great Ancestors of the Wing Chun system.

Samuel Kwok

In my early days training, like a lot of students practicing Wing Chun, I found it difficult to relax when practicing the form. Sigung's advice was simple: "don't use brute force."

Jim Fung

The most important things are motivation, self-discipline, and timing. You should love what you are doing, care about what you are doing, and have compassion for yourself and for others.

Francis Fong

One might say the style has been modernized also because time has passed, and people have added new ways of looking at the art and its applications.

Augustine Fong

The most important qualities for students to become proficient in Wing Chun are serious and consistent dedication to hard training.

Alan Lee

In Wing Chun, the aim is always to counter an attack with an even more effective one, so the Wing Chun response is very offensive in nature.

David Peterson

I believe there are styles that complement the development as a WT practitioner and others that are counter-productive. BJJ in my opinion is a great addition to WT because it covers the ground fighting aspect while WT is extremely powerful as a stand-up system.

Thommy L. Boehlig

Without health, you will be unable to use Kung Fu in self-defense. It is good to understand the culture and tradition, but this again is not as important as one's health.

Ip Chun

I was lucky and was able to study many wing chun systems in the Yip Man family, but I concentrated on studying more of what Hawkins Cheung taught me. Hawkins' style I feel is unique, his wing chun emphasizes body structure and stresses combat applications.

Robert Chu

As far as Chi Sao in relation to application and real combat, well there are only two guarantees in street self-defense: Contact and movement. It is those two elements that are the basis of Chi Sao.

Shaun Rawcliffe

The Wing Chun system is very popular, however the standard is very inconsistent. What my father taught has been diluted in many cases and the integrity of Ip Man's Wing Chun is in danger of disappearing if we cannot standardize his teachings.

Ip Ching

Each martial arts style or system goes into battle believing it has all the answers. Any classical style deals with the imparting of a fixed knowledge that becomes alive when it is mastered.

Hawkins Cheung

I adhere to the traditional values and the 'traditional' principle of using what it works. In order to do that, a constant modification and experimentation is required to catch up with the times.

Emin Boztepe

Wing Chun was never meant to be a sport, and learning rules etc. dilutes the street skills in my humble opinion.

Shaun Rawcliffe

Seek out a good teacher, train hard and concentrate on learning the basic skills very well.

David Peterson

I have a problem with methods that do not translate well from the training floor to the violent street encounter. There are a lot of things that work with a compliant training partner that won't come close to working against a violent street predator.

Tony Massengill

I strongly believe that each martial art should be a complete system based on specific principles and training goals. Therefore, I do not think that mixing kung fu styles is beneficial to the student.

William Kwok

The overall importance of ground fighting skills has been almost universally acknowledged and is now a part of the training regimen of nearly all true combat-minded martial artists.

Randy Williams

Learning the forms properly, practicing them diligently, and understanding them thoroughly are the three essential steps towards a successful wing chun experience.

Jim Lau

We teach, we learn, and we promote traditional Chinese Martial Arts. We are all one big Kung Fu family on four seas and six continents.

Lin Xiang Fuk

Chinese people always say, "You always learn as you live longer." I also tell my students: Wing Chun is your life, and your life is Wing Chun. We learn from our life and a lot of life experience can also reflect Wing Chun training.

Gorden Lu

In Wing Chun, we assume that we are weaker, smaller, and slower than our opponents; therefore, we must have a clever way to overcome a more powerful adversary.

Alan Lee

A teacher can only guide you. He cannot work or think for you. Guidance, however, should not be underestimated.

Jim Lau

Students learn for two or three years and start comparing their skills to other arts on the Internet. Some also want to follow trends. What they fail to understand is that Wing Chun is not an art that can be learned overnight.

Gary Lam

Self-defense has nothing to do with a strength and conditioning program involving weights, running, stretching, etc.

Leung Ting

For me, wing chun is a skill. If you describe it as an art, there is no way to determine if it is effective or not.

Wong Shun Leung

A strong mindset is just as important. It involves the ability to set clear goals and keep them in your mind at all times. A martial artist with a strong mindset is not discouraged by setbacks, but instead sees them as opportunities for improvement. A positive attitude, mental toughness and the ability to overcome obstacles are crucial elements of a strong mindset.

Mohammed Ince

Choose the right teacher; this will save you years in your training. Find a teacher who not only will allow you to ask questions but will encourage you to do so.

Samuel Kwok

The Wing Chun system is like a chain, and for that chain to be strong, it cannot have any weak links. The system is very articulate. To be really good at it, you must build up every joint and muscle, working body and mind in harmony.

Jim Fung

Wing Chun has good fundamentals, and I believe that it can help individuals grow mentally, physically, and spiritually. It definitely has helped me. Wing Chun focuses on reflex training and sensitivity—your timing, your response to the situation.

Francis Fong

The key to starting training in Wing Chun is to do your research; remember that web sites, "YouTube" videos and the equivalent that promote a martial art school are put up there by those doing the promoting, so are not necessarily honest or legitimate. My advice is be discerning; go watch a lesson or two, be respectful, but ask the questions that matter and see if you feel comfortable in that environment.

Shaun Rawcliffe

When I studied with Sifu Hawkins Cheung, I found that the real DNA of wing chun is body structure, and this is what permeates in the application of it. What I was lacking in my previous study was how to use body power.

Robert Chu

PHILOSOPHY

Real Kung Fu was and still is a Martial system. A method of beating the opponent in a real and violent encounter.

Ip Ching

An instructor should never train less of that what he expects from his students. Training is training regardless of your level of skill.

Emin Boztepe

As far as the training goes, I always incorporate a combination of traditional and modern teaching methods, so that the students are comfortable with both methods. Each way has merit, and each way gets good results.

David Peterson

Every expert has to find a way to make his movements simple, direct and economical. If you have a lot of fundamental movements, you have to test out each movement to discover how to refine them and make them simple, direct and economical.

Hawkins Cheung

I don't believe I will ever stop learning or improving. My teaching skills alone have developed and improved over time considerably.

Shaun Rawcliffe

Train with reality at the forefront at all times, taking care of your partner's improvement and safety at all times. If your partner improves, you will too, so it is in your own interest to make sure that he or she is given all the best possible opportunities to develop.

David Peterson

Unfortunately, the Martial Arts in general seem to be dominated by a sporting mind-set. I believe this is bad for the Martial Arts. We are losing so much of the real art by focusing on sport.

Tony Massengill

I believe that only through teaching can one practice and reach the highest goals of martial arts understanding.

Jim Lau

Why would everyone want to do everything the same? There must be differing slants on each art, and students will tend to gravitate towards the approach that suits them the best.

Randy Williams

I studied Wing Chun not only because I like the art, but also as a personal mission for me, to keep Wing Chun instruction direct from the family and to follow the family tradition.

Gorden Lu

Students get involved with too many activities and give all kinds of excuses for not attending every class, so the quality of Wing Chun is diminishing.

Alan Lee

A Wing Tsun practitioner will close the gap and will powerfully attack the opponent's head, disturbing his balance and preventing any kicking action of actually taking place.

Leung Ting

It is not a matter of likes or dislikes—the skills can be proved. So I look at wing chun more as a skill than an art. Taken in that context, there's nothing wrong with using your skills if you have to.

Wong Shun Leung

Competitions are effective training tools, but it should always be remembered that they have rules. In a true life-threatening situation, there are no rules. That is why Chi Sau is so important.

Samuel Kwok

I have so much respect for Sigung Tsui, not just as my master but as a person as well. He is very private and humble—he never boasts about his ability—and I have learned a lot from his philosophy of life, his way of dealing with people.

Jim Fung

Teaching has certainly played a huge role in my personal development because when you stand out the front and have to instruct, to answer the questions and provide individual solutions and coaching, your own level of understanding and expertise increases tremendously.

David Peterson

It is very important to have positive energy. Attitude will determine your behavior. I always tell my students, "Try doesn't work."

Francis Fong

As long as one is alive, there is always room for improvement. That is the wonderful thing about training Kung Fu, there is always something you can improve by training.

Ip Chun

You have to leave techniques and theory behind and really dig deep to reveal the principles and concepts behind your systems. That is real training.

Robert Chu

If your opponent is fast, you be slow. If he is slow, you be fast. You must always keep in control of a fighting situation.

Hawkins Cheung

Fighting is not only done with the fist but also with other qualities such as dedication, perseverance, focus, et cetera. And as you probably guessed, I'm not talking about a physical confrontation.

Emin Boztepe

In an attempt to provide explanations that suit the different learning styles of my students, I have differentiated my teaching, providing explanations through auditory, visual and kinesthetic means.

Shaun Rawcliffe

I believe that people are getting a little more open with sharing and working together. The politics is still pretty bad, but I believe it is getting better.

Tony Massengill

When you feel the confrontation is inevitable, don't hesitate —attack!

Leung Ting

Our aim is never to "Chi Sau" with our opponent, but should a situation occur where the limbs are trapped, jammed, grabbed, dragged or obstructed in any way, "Chi Sau" instills the necessary reflexes and reactions to deal with these issues and allow us to continue to attack whilst keeping our enemy in check.

David Peterson

The real martial artists are out there training and getting the job done, not just constantly chatting about it on the Net. And if the real guys have a beef with you, you'll know about it, not read about it.

Randy Williams

There are many details and ideas in each Wing Chun form, but there always are a few key things that represent each form that the practitioner needs to pay more attention to.

Gorden Lu

I look for students with the right mental attitude and approach. I don't want to equip bullies and idiots with greater tools than they already have.

Shaun Rawcliffe

The "Baat Jaam Do" ("eight-slash knives") not only teaches an effec- tive means of utilizing a short weapon, either singularly or a pair, but it is also able to enhance the strength of the wrists and stance in a similar way to the pole form.

David Peterson

No martial art is perfect. Each has a specialty or different approach to fighting.

Alan Lee

PHILOSOPHY

Today, I still live by the ancient Chinese proverb that says, "The person who teaches will learn himself, and the person who learns will always be the teacher of himself."

Jim Lau

I encourage all qualified instructors to teach from the heart to those who want to learn the art. Don't keep any secrets. Let's make the art flourish for many generations to come.

Carson Lau

Bruce was totally aware that jeet kune do is very hard to do because it depends on the student's capabilities. This can be really confusing for the students, especially if they lack a strong base and deep understanding.

Wong Shun Leung

There are instructors who have trained in a seminar or two with Grandmasters Ip Chun and/or Ip Ching, and now claim their lineage as being through them. They mislead students as to their lineage and their depth of knowledge.

Samuel Kwok

In the beginning, my main emphasis was on self-defense. Wing Chun appealed because I found I could learn it quickly and apply it straight away. Now, I regard it more as an art, and as with any true art, there is no limit to your learning.

Jim Fung

I think it is the practitioner who cultivates his martial art is most important. In the end, everyone develops his own personal style and if he has followers, a "school" ensues.

Robert Chu

Talent is not everything. If people have negative energy and a negative attitude, they never will succeed, no matter what they do in life. They blame other people for their failures or blame it on something instead of taking responsibility for their actions.

Francis Fong

Once a student has finished learning one style, he can get involved with another. Without a total understanding of at least one style, a student might just end up with chop-suey.

Alan Lee

Wing Chun is not a style, but a system of preparation for combat. Wing Chun gives you the information to be one step ahead of your opponent.

Hawkins Cheung

You have to find a way or style you like and learn how to use it in many different situations. There are certain principles or methods that can be interchanged but you have to be careful since you may end up 'confusing' your own body.

Emin Boztepe

I think Wing Chun is going through a huge evolution. On the one hand various "new versions" of Wing Chun are emerging from little known and sometime tenuously linked families.

Shaun Rawcliffe

The Wing Chun forms are cleverly designed to teach both techniques and concepts.

David Peterson

I do believe some people train Chi Sao improperly and allow it to become a competition. This is a mistake and robs the student of the true benefit of Chi Sao training. The other problem is that often Wing Chun people mistake Chi Sao skill for fighting skill.

Tony Massengill

Although your father may have taught you to speak, I still know it's you on the phone when you call and not your father. I believe martial arts is the same.

Randy Williams

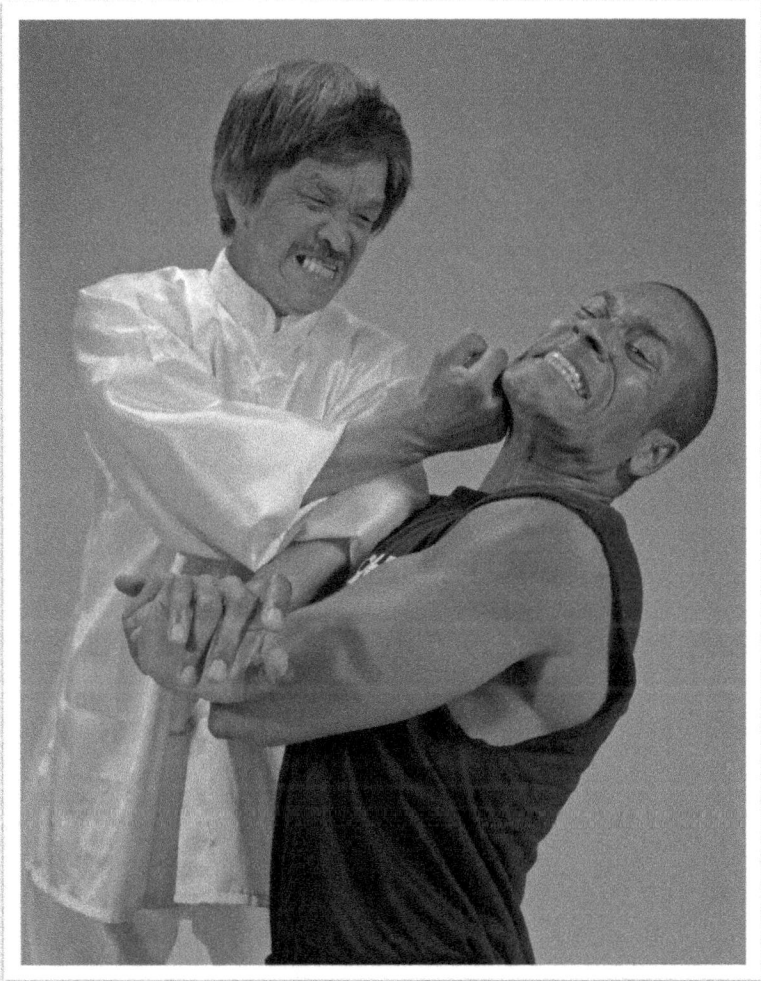

Communication is a form of influence, and the ability to properly influence someone without having to use physical capabilities is an art within martial arts.

Jim Lau

The commercialization of martial arts has also contributed to the changes in martial arts culture. Unfortunately, some schools today focus solely on attracting students and making a profit, rather than on upholding traditional values and practices. This can lead to a dilution of the true essence of martial arts.

William Kwok

The first form is more abstract and needs a lot of understanding and imagination. Most movements are teaching the position, structure, and the ideas behind the move. The second and third forms have more applications techniques involved.

Gorden Lu

I do think that there are still "pure" styles of Kung Fu, including Wing Chun, so long as the core concepts of these systems have remained unchanged.

David Peterson

When you learn the art of Wing Tsun or any other martial art for that matter, you are learning fighting techniques, but this is not a reason to bully others and to be arrogant about it.

Leung Ting

Different styles may suit different individuals. Some styles are more energetic, focus on relaxation, or focus on the street scenario applications. It also depends on the stature, age, and goal of the student (more athletic, more health-oriented, self-defense related).

Samuel Kwok

Students must also be prepared to put time into their training and realize that while they are able to learn techniques quickly, mastery only comes with years of practice.

Jim Fung

Sifu Hawkins Cheung said it's the application that counts the most. In other schools people always care if they were passed down the art correctly, but I find even if it is transmitted "correctly," but if one cannot make it work, it's worthless.

Robert Chu

By applying the principles of Yin-Yang theory with Wing Chun, I seek balance and harmony between opposing forces in my practice. This balance extends beyond my martial arts training and helps me adapt to change in my life.

William Kwok

The goal of any legitimate combat system is the incapacitation of the opponent, so overall it is fair to say that all good systems have that in common, even if the specific methods differ.

David Peterson

Wing Chun is not better than other systems of martial arts, but it offers a practitioner some unique advantages. No matter what style or system of martial arts, to defeat your opponent you must land your tools.

Hawkins Cheung

For me the most important goal is inner peace. Martial arts is a journey into yourself and it is form of research and introspection especially through the hard times.

Emin Boztepe

In order to succeed at anything in life, you have to love what you are doing, have compassion for yourself and others, and the conviction to put in the time and effort to achieve your goal.

Francis Fong

The Baat Cham Dao form consists of a systematic set of movements and techniques that utilize the essential footwork, positions and structures of the Wing Chun system.

Shaun Rawcliffe

There needs to be a balance in all aspects of training. Just training forms or just doing "Chi Sau" or just sparring—none of those alone will make you a complete fighter.

David Peterson

The Chinese speak of the trinity of motion, Body + Step + Hand. These three must be coordinated in order for your kung fu to have power.

Tony Massengill

Whether we want to believe it or not, almost all systems are modified through the years, even if inadvertently. It can be compared to learning your mother language from parents-you can't help but add your own personal flavor to the language when you speak it.

Randy Williams

Many confuse Wing Chun with other martial arts without understanding Wing Chun's ideas, and they create a kind of chop suey. I don't blame other martial artists who laugh at Wing Chun.

Alan Lee

At the core of wing chun maneuvers is the concept of the centerline, the imaginary vertical line running down the center of the body—in front and back.

Jim Lau

Wing Chun is a mental, rather than physical martial art. The system was created by a lady and as a result, the art requires mental strategy and physical skill and timing. Wing Chun requires that the mental be ahead of the physical. It is a system to develop skill, not a style.

Hawkins Cheung

If you see that you can't avoid the fight, then initiate the attack as fast as you can and try to defeat your aggressor powerfully, without giving him a second chance.

Leung Ting

I have taught Wing Chun in many different countries and have noticed that westerners respond to traditional Chinese training in different ways. Europe, people more look into the spiritual, health and skills. In America, people are more interested in the fighting techniques, along with quick results and strength.

Gorden Lu

I think the standard is high, according to my Masters Ip Chun and Ip Ching; however, Hong Kong remains the highest standard. The grandmasters are based in Hong Kong.

Samuel Kwok

The most important quality is understanding how the system works. I have devised a training program that teaches students from the first day step by step the logic and scientific reasoning of each technique.

Jim Fung

Personally, I think it is despicable when people lie and talk about their made-up origins as real, but if a style has merits, then I try to focus on that.

Robert Chu

The development of the tremendous forearm and wrist strength required by the Pole form benefits Wing Chun's punching power in addition to some of the basic hand techniques.

Shaun Rawcliffe

Wing Chun is a combat skill designed for attack.

David Peterson

Try to study with as many people in your field as possible and concentrate on that. Then, get perspectives from outside your area of expertise.

Robert Chu

I have been involved in the Martial Arts for over 50-plus years and Wing Chun is the best system I have found for my needs. I encourage students to search around.

Tony Massengill

No one owns a style of martial arts they didn't create. Thus, no one can tell you that you can't use the movements of your style in any given way.

Randy Williams

Most Chinese people know learning Kung Fu is not an easy thing to do, and they also know it takes time, and tremendous patience.

Gorden Lu

Who I am is not important. Who I learned from is not important. The most important thing is whether what I have learned is practical.

Alan Lee

Once contact is made with the opponent's arms, he can be effectively maneuvered by adhering to the wing chun motto: "When hands approach, withhold. When hands withdraw, follow. And when hands slip from control, strike."

Jim Lau

Developments in sports science, particularly in strength & conditioning, healthier diet and safer ways to exercise, has provided us with the means to enhance what we do, but has not forced any- one to abandon the "purity" of the arts.

David Peterson

It is my conviction that training kung fu is a form of personal development. Kung fu training confronts you with yourself, with your negative character trades, your limitations and weaknesses. It strips you of every fake mask and brings your true character into the foreground.

Thommy L. Boehlig

Now, my practice of kung fu has become a calling, a path towards greater self-awareness, personal growth, and spiritual enlightenment. It's not just about fighting or self-defense anymore—it's a way of life.

William Kwok

TECHNIQUE

All physical and mental tension must be discarded, the natural instinct to resist and tense, even lock the muscles under pressure must be trained out, as must the desire to use brute strength when applying techniques.

Shaun Rawcliffe

For Wing Chun, the long range is actually a kind of pre-fighting range and is not our preferred fighting platform. This is because one of Wing Chun's strengths is hand and arm sensitivity, so in order to maximize this advantage we need to get into contact with our opponent's arms.

Donald Mak

People are becoming increasingly aware that there are different approaches to the Wing Chun system and that not all branches of the tree are the same.

David Peterson

Siu Lim Tao lays the groundwork for how to move your body, position yourself and be aware of your surroundings, among other skills. Chum Kiu shows you how to apply some of the Siu Lim Tao techniques from different angles, as well as how to turn, balance, twist, step, kick and approach an opponent. Biu Tze teaches you advanced and more offensive techniques.

Carson Lau

The eye is too slow to recognize an action and pick a proper response fast enough to keep us from getting hurt at such a close distance. It works in much the same way as maintaining a safe following distance when driving. You need "reaction time," the sense of touch, and the development that takes place in Chi Sao.

Tony Massengill

In my classes, I place great emphasis on students understanding both the movements of the forms and their application. We move directly from form to application to teach students how to use the techniques in a real attack scenario. This is followed by sparring to solidify the movements and develop a deep understanding of their application.

Mohammed Ince

With the abundance of instructional materials available today, virtually anyone with an earnest desire to learn wing chun can do so with relative ease.

Randy Williams

Cross-training is essential for every martial art, but it is important to understand that one should not overdo it.

Kim Man Chan

In HKB system, we don't focus on muscle development; instead, we focus on tendons.

Lin Xiang Fuk

I love to use supplementary training methods and I found that can always benefit my students on learning and using Wing Chun.

Gorden Lu

Sticky hands is one part of the syllabus learned before training how to fight. Unfortunately, some people erroneously think if they practice sticky hands long enough, they can fight using sticky hands.

Alan Lee

By incorporating stretching into their routine, students can increase their flexibility and range of motion, reduce their risk of injury, improve posture and body alignment, relieve muscle tension and soreness, and even promote relaxation.

William Kwok

Chi sao is like learning a song. You learn the notes and lyrics, and then you put the song together.

Jim Lau

All three forms are interrelated. Again, Siu Nin Tao is the alphabet, Chum Kiu and Biu Jee are the words. In chi-sao practice, you learn to put them together and make sentences.

Gary Lam

Overall, wing chun stresses counter-fighting techniques, the emphasis being on neutralization.

Alan Lamb

In Wing Tsun we don't look to grab or grapple with the opponent. The main idea is not to make your body "hard" but keep it 'soft', re-borrowing the pulling force from the aggressor and hit back before the grappler can actually deliver his technique.

Leung Ting

What counts in real combat is determination, courage, and vigor. If you're superior in these aspects, then you can often knock down your opponent with two or three simple techniques.

Wong Shun Leung

Running is very good for aerobic and anaerobic training for full-contact fighting, and weights can be useful, depending on the type of training; for example, training the biceps and triceps muscles. Be careful and avoid "bulking up" the upper body muscles. Training should focus on your forms and Chi Sao.

Samuel Kwok

I learned how to teach these two styles by following Ip Man's teaching curriculum and that is the biggest difference to most people who teach in the current time that they only emphasize one style.

Gorden Lu

In internal Wing Tsun it is fundamentally important not to execute specific movements by intent, but rather to explore the environment with movement and attentiveness to perceive current "arguments."

Keith R. Kernspecht

The complete Ving Tsun system uses two weapons which are the butterfly knives and the long pole. The long pole was used in a large space against multiple opponents while the butterfly knives are short-range weapons.

Victor Kan

Technical changes do not make a system "un-pure," they merely help to make a system more effective, both to train and to apply.

David Peterson

Once you have a good foundation from training with the three empty hand forms, you will find the practical application in Chi Sao is relatively easy. This is because the techniques and movements are the same.

Jim Fung

In Wing Chun, there are only three empty-hand forms: Siu Nim Tao, Chum Kiu, and Bil Gee. None is more advanced or deadly than the other.

Alan Lee

Learning different styles of martial arts can help one understand the unique characteristics of each style in combat, allowing for a better understanding of martial arts as a whole.

Kim Man Chan

Wing Tsun focuses on close, quick strikes and techniques that aim to precisely strike the core of the opponent's body, thereby defeating him quickly. One of the most fascinating aspects of this style is its philosophy of using the opponent's strength against himself.

Mohammed Ince

Chi sao, or sticking hands practice, is the final wing chun training method. This drill is used to sharpen and condition one's instinctive fighting responses.

Jim Lau

In Wing Chun, learn the basics – learn proper position and understand structure. You cannot just do it; you have to understand it.

Francis Fong

From the Wing Chun point of view, punching with excessive strength results in a great deal of power remaining in the arm. This inhibits the instantaneous release of power.

Augustine Fong

Chi Sao is the glue that binds the forms to the application in fighting. Chi Sao teaches the student when and how to use energy, and how to overcome the opponents force with the proper use of angles.

Ip Chun

In Wing Chun, there are three empty- hand forms and a Wooden Dummy form. All the Wing Chun techniques are from those four forms. Chi-sao is the application of the forms. Beginners should spend more time on the forms. Advanced practitioners should spend more time on chi-sao.

Chung Kwok Chow

Sticking hands should be practiced and played as a "game," in the same way that Tiger cubs learn to "kill" without using their claws during the learning process.

Shaun Rawcliffe

My advice to students regarding supplementary training is to focus on their primary training instead of looking for additional training. Wing Chun is a complete martial arts system that includes forms, long pole, butterfly knives, and qigong, providing a well-rounded practice.

William Kwok

If a martial artist is close-minded, he will never have greatness in his expression of the art.

Robert Chu

If you are train for sport, you cannot expect to respond appropriately in a violent street encounter.

Tony Massengill

The most important point for a student to become proficient is that of patience. They must thoroughly learn the method and underlying principles of each step, and not rush on to more advanced training than they are ready for.

Ip Ching

While I thoroughly enjoy cross-training and the experience of being a new learner again and again, not to mention the extended knowledge that it brings to my experience, for me it is WSLVT that answers all my questions and is what works best for me.

David Peterson

The Butterfly Knife technique we call Bart Cham Dao, it is unique to our style and is regarded as a jewel of the Wing Chun system.

Stephen Chan

Speed and power were his greatest assets but even the level of those would decrease over the years and Bruce would definitely compensate with other attributes in order to keep his level up.

William Cheung

Lien wan kuen is a major application of the Wing Chun principle, each one of your shots scores and sets up for the next shot. You do not give your opponent a chance to breathe.

Hawkins Cheung

Forms are important to teach and reinforce proper structure, alignment, angle, and Yiu Ma (waist energy) development.

Tony Massengill

The form Siu Lim Tao mainly focuses on stance, relaxation, hand position, structure, and power generation. Chum Kiu emphasizes turning, weight transfer, footwork, stepping, and isolating the stance using your upper body in order to produce more power when you are moving. And the last empty hand form, Bil Jee, focuses on elbow strikes, opponent take- downs, learning how to defend and attack from multiple angles, using up and down body positions, etc.

Au Yeung

Definitely there is an evolution in the technical part of any art but also this change in increased by the practitioner maturity process and personal experience. You perception and understanding of a basic punch or technique changes with your level of education and expertise in the art. You may find new ways of doing some techniques, but it doesn't necessary you change the art.

Emin Boztepe

Weight training can, if someone doesn't fully understand the result of their actions, be detrimental. I would never say do not weight train, join a gym or do other exercises, but I would get them to consider the pros and cons of that training in regards to their Wing Chun development.

Shaun Rawcliffe

Through "Chi Sau" we are taught how to "read" the opponent's intentions and to counter those intentions instantaneously with actions that control and hit the opponent.

David Peterson

To truly master a martial art, it is essential to focus on its principles and gain a deep understanding of the system.

William Kwok

Chi Sao is the bridge between the forms and application in fighting. Chi Sao teaches very important elements such as sensitivity, relaxation under stress, and proper structure in technique.

Tony Massengill

My rationale is this: if two guys are the same size and skill level, the stronger and fitter one will win nine times out of ten, so it just makes sense to be the strongest and fittest you can be.

Randy Williams

During a real fight, you must consider every aspect of survival. Therefore, "skill challenge" is an important part of training. It is one of the ways to validate how the body responds under stress.

Lin Xiang Fuk

One of the biggest challenges in Wing Chun is how to get close to your opponent and capitalize on its close-range fighting capabilities.

Donald Mak

The correct way of practice Kung Fu is not just doing the same move over and over. You should have a training plan, right tools, and a systematic and supporting exercises program.

Gorden Lu

Sticky hands (chi sao) is just a way of training to use some of the hand movements correctly, combine the different hand movements together, coverage, reflex, and improve your techniques and combinations.

Alan Lee

Chi sao helps you build hand sensitivity-and that's basically the idea, to develop that instantaneous reflex to reach without thinking, because when you talk about movement, your eyes can- not be as fast as your mind.

Jim Lau

Wing Chun is such a high-level art that it's like a chess game. It's a very deep art and there are different approaches to each situation. There's a counter to every move, and this makes the art interesting.

Gary Lam

People's lifestyles differ, their backgrounds differ, as do their experiences, personality, talent, body size, etc.—That's why a lot of people teach the same style, but the techniques are different.

Gorden Lu

My students are only taught the pole when their training in the basic empty hand techniques is complete.

Jim Fung

The first form, Siu Lim Tao, is the most important—it has the basic positions and stance. For example, tan sau, fok sau and the centerline theory. This form focuses on how to train for power and energy.

Samuel Kwok

Paul Lam's Chi Sau was more physical, with a heavy emphasis on push-pull techniques. Koo Sang's chi sau was a lot softer, and he emphasized more counter-fighting techniques.

Alan Lamb

Don't kick above the waist even of your ability allows it and make sure your foot travels straight and directly to the target without a chambering action as it can be seen in other martial arts systems.

Leung Ting

Wing Tsun emphasizes the development of body control, speed, and responsiveness. Rather than relying solely on pure physical strength, this martial art focuses on using one's body efficiently and targeting the opponent's anatomical and physiological weak points.

Mohammed Ince

Chi sao is very important in wing chun, but too much emphasis is placed on the idea of "sticking" to the hands- this causes the student to end up chasing the hands instead of punching and trapping.

Wong Shun Leung

In internal Wing Tsun we do not want to learn the exercises (form techniques), but rather learn "with the help" of the exercises (form techniques). As exercises the solo forms help us to unite ourselves into a "wedge" and a "ball".

Keith R. Kernspecht

The weapons in Wing Tsun provide a different dynamic in weapon training than just using empty hands. Besides the strength benefits from gripping the weapons, you also have to deal with different range and distance when facing an opponent.

Carson Lau

Correct application of Chi Sao can control the movements of your opponent and cut down his angles of attack.

Samuel Kwok

Ving Tsun's two basic foot techniques are a front kick and a side kick. Both are delivered through the centerline of the body and strike home with the heel.

Victor Kan

I would strongly recommend a student spend the majority of his or her training time on the three empty hand forms then moving on to Chi Sao, wall bag and Muk Yan Jong in that order.

Jim Fung

The ideas behind weapons training come from the empty-hand techniques, but they are modified to fit fights with weapons and add a lot more "gung lek" training.

Alan Lee

In my experience, students are drawn to kung fu primarily for its self-defense techniques, and they expect to learn practical skills that they can apply in real-life situations.

William Kwok

In the beginning, you have to work on form. It's important to focus on foundation and basics—form, drill, and application. Form is structure and sequence. Drilling provides repetition of technique. Application is understanding when to execute the technique.

Francis Fong

The empty hand forms lay the structural foundation for the Wing Chun system. Each one builds on the foundation laid by the previous form.

Ip Ching

In my classes I teach first how to make the right structure for each one of the Chi Sao moves. Then, the correct point of contact.

Augustine Fong

The ability to record training on video is a great advantage for the students nowadays. Years ago, this was not possible, so we had to rely on our memory.

Ip Chun

Weapons are the extension and enhancer of hands. The long pole is for long range, while butterfly knives are best for close range. They are two completely unrelated skills. The pole is single-headed and relies on both hands to manipulate, while butterfly knives are manipulated by one hand and can be used individually or in a pair. Long poles were used by them for paddling and pushing the boat. They are not very practical on land. Butterfly knives can execute techniques just as the hands can.

Chung Kwok Chow

Speed, strength, accuracy, timing and cruelty are the basic requirements to get the job done, and a student has to learn how to apply things under stress. I think free fighting is just a means to develop proficiency under stress, but it is not everything.

Robert Chu

Wing Chun is a trap too, because many practitioners get hung up thinking Wing Chun is the only way to fight.

Hawkins Cheung

Many students use too much muscular strength and turn Chi Sao into a wrestling match rather than the reaction and sensitivity exercise it is designed to be.

Ip Ching

I have developed the ability to identify and communicate the "keys" of the core principles of the Wing Chun Style.

Samuel Kwok

You might have Bruce's physical technique but lack the knowledge he had to make it work. So, what's the use of trying to copy him?

William Cheung

We come to the Wing Chun six-and-a-half-point pole. I would suggest that the pole has no relation whatsoever to the Wing Chun family fighting system at all or to the Wing Chun family.

Stephen Chan

Siu Lim Tao is the most important form in the system. It develops Chi Kung, your Chi, and your physical power all at once and in one single form. You can learn the movements in one single day but to really understand and digest the true principles and applications of the concepts intrinsic to the form, takes a very long time.

Augustine Fong

The Wooden Dummy form is a very important training tool in Ving Tsun. It helps practitioners to further coordinate their hand and footwork, and to attack and defend from different angles in a consistent manner.

Kim Man Chan

When I first started training kung fu, I was only able to use my hand to block or attack from a certain distance. Over the years, I have learned to understand that we have to be able to use any part of our body to defend or attack. In addition, I realized we cannot just master one form of fighting or be happy to fight just within one particular range.

Au Yeung

I don't want to hurt the feelings of other practitioners, but if you look at karate, for example, you use outside blocks while we in wing tsun stress the importance of protecting the body to a much greater extent. We focus on protecting all of the vital, living organs of the body. I carry a passion for wing tsun and I think people feel this when I teach.

Emin Boztepe

The Muk Yan Chong training is crucial for the skill development of a Wing Chun student. The form includes techniques from the three unarmed forms, which students can mix and practice on the dummy.

William Kwok

It is this close quarter proximity that Chi Sao practice aims to imitate, control and dominate. Through correct continuous practice and training, Chi Sao develops the skills and abilities to enable Wing Chun practitioners to respond quickly.

Shaun Rawcliffe

Styles or systems do not necessarily complement each other, with some being diametrically opposed to each other both physically and conceptually.

David Peterson

The problem I see with the mixing of systems is that the student ends up being "a mile wide but only an inch deep" in his or her knowledge.

Tony Massengill

Go for real; experience it; try it to find out what is true. This is what we call applied Wing Chun.

Alan Lee

A martial artist cannot afford to be lazy. To be a good student, and eventually a good teacher, takes many, many hours of hard work and many gallons of sweat.

Randy Williams

It's very important to choose the right qualified teacher who is willing to teach with his or her whole heart. But they can be anywhere, not just Hong Kong and China or Taiwan.

Lin Xiang Fuk

Wing Chun is very flexible and sometimes is very easy to adapt to other styles. You may not need to really learn the style; you just need to learn the right techniques.

Gorden Lu

In Wing Chun we have another term for free sparring-we call it *lut sao*. This is a situation where there will be a defender and an attacker, and the attacker will attempt to keep the defender near his range, while the defender will make every attempt to keep him away.

Jim Lau

I had the opportunity to test my Wing Chun skills against various martial artists and I had to adapt to different opponents.

Gary Lam

No one in Yip Man wing chun fights exactly the same as Yip Man did—it is not a style that you learn to fight with and duplicate your master.

Robert Chu

In Wing Chun, the long pole and butterfly knives are two popular weapons that are considered to be related to empty hands training. The benefits of weapons training can have a positive impact on a student's empty hand abilities.

William Kwok

I was constantly being tested by both Koo Sang and the students. During chi sau practice, they would constantly throw me fresh guys to practice with.

Alan Lamb

All the forms all come together in the training of Chi Sao. Chi Sao is the bridge between forms and fighting. Chi Sao is the skill of Wing Chun.

Ip Ching

The "advanced" techniques are those we use in a real fight. There are no 'secret' moves or applications that will defeat any other technique.

Leung Ting

Bruce didn't get to see the best part of wing chun during his early days of training under Yip Man. He then came back to Hong Kong, and truly learned the foundation of what would eventually become his own style.

Wong Shun Leung

Chi Sao, if done properly, teaches you how to react automatically. Chi Sao is a special technique and training method used in Wing Chun.

Samuel Kwok

The only limit is the limit of one's mind and understanding.

Shaun Rawcliffe

The Wing Tsun that is generally known: It is arm-biased, mainly linear, bases itself on a "wedge" and works with what some American scientists call "automatisms."

Keith R. Kernspecht

Right after "qor sao," the student moves on to learn Chum Kiu. This is basically a defensive form, teaching students how to turn and simultaneously block in response to attacks and then immediately counter them.

Victor Kan

Muk Yan Jong (wooden dummy) takes the place of a sparring partner, and is taught at the end of empty hand training, because most of the wooden dummy techniques arise from the three empty-hand forms.

Jim Fung

As far as the forms are concerned, they need to be practiced regularly and not discarded early on in the training or rushed through occasionally.

David Peterson

Bil Jee is very important in that it trains you how to recover your center-line in an "emergency" situation (provide an illustration of this concept). You train to use two energies going in different directions, in that you borrow the energy of your opponent and use many elbow techniques.

Samuel Kwok

Wing Chun's power comes from your legs and body, together with your arms to form as one piece, which allows you to generate linear momentum and angular momentum in fighting.

Donald Mak

Cross-training can help you to understand yourself better. You have to discover what is suitable for you, as well as for a particular situation. Focus on yourself.

Francis Fong

The Chi Sao motions are what make the forms. Forms are the textbooks as far as the right and correct way of doing the movement, but Chi Sao will tell you how to apply them—like a laboratory for the techniques you have learned in the three empty hand forms.

Augustine Fong

The third form (Bil Jee) teaches how to generate and extend the power from the shoulder. This form also combined the first two forms' ideas, hand movements, and footwork, and emphasizes open and longer fighting distance applications.

Gorden Lu

Forms build technique and structure. Chi Sao trains the use of technique, structure and sensitivity. I believe both are equally important to one's training.

Ip Chun

Because of their culture, Chinese kung fu practitioners can pick up certain concepts or moves quicker than European or American practitioners. On the other hand, Europeans and Americans usually have bigger builds, so they have better physical capabilities.

Chung Kwok Chow

The weapons skills are a complement to the empty hand skills. They teach you how to move with weight and how to dynamically apply your power and momentum through an apparatus.

Robert Chu

Bruce became very analytical, very scientific. If something doesn't make sense with scientific logic, it must be wrong. He also did a lot of research on physical conditioning. Just look at the screen—he had a great physical appearance.

William Cheung

The staff and knife are weapons that come with serious legal responsibilities in today's society, and they are rarely used. However, as weapons in Ving Tsun, training with the staff greatly enhances the muscular strength of the arms, waist, and legs of the practitioner.

Kim Man Chan

Every martial arts student has to solve the problem of applying the physical portion. All martial arts styles tend to be theoretical in application. Bruce may have abandoned some Wing Chun tools, but he didn't abandon Wing Chun development.

Hawkins Cheung

The first form Siu Lim Tao is fundamental to everything else. You have to start off with fundamentals. It is a stationary form that teaches the student the basics of special breathing exercises like internal strength, etc.

Stephen Chan

The three hand forms are like a database of all the techniques in Wing Chun, but Chi Sao is like a writing program to identify the solution from the database.

Au Yeung

I have never found it necessary to mix anything with Wing Chun.

Ip Ching

The third form, Biu Gee, teaches the student the power of relaxation in application of technique. Here they will learn about Whipping Energy and recovery from a lost position.

Ip Ching

My anti-grappling is based on the WT concepts and works fantastic for the average person and even for someone who is a wrestler or grappler.

Emin Boztepe

You must try the techniques with people who are really punching or kicking at you to learn the technique and make it work.

Alan Lee

It is important to understand why Chi Sao is beneficial, where it fits into the training process and how it applies in self-defense.

Shaun Rawcliffe

Far too many Martial Arts practitioners blame the system that they are practicing for their failures, when what they should be doing is asking, "What did I do wrong?"

David Peterson

The reason why I started teaching is because right before leaving Hong Kong I went to visit my Sifu, and he told me that I should find someone to teach so I could practice my Chi Sao. So, the main purpose was so I could just keep up my training. I was not looking for students or to make money from it.

Augustine Fong

We react the way we are trained. That is the reason for training, to develop reaction. It's called "conditioned reflex." That is the goal of Martial Art training.

Tony Massengill

Although some empty-hand techniques are used with the knives and they are seen as extensions of your limbs, you have to be very careful that they are sharp tools, and one mistake can be fatal or even deadly.

Carson Lau

The first and foremost purpose of kung-fu is self-defense. That doesn't just mean protecting yourself against bullies who want to beat you up, it also involves defending yourself by using your head in your training to avoid injury when you can.

Randy Williams

The weaponry skills are definitely related to the empty-hand skill. In HKB, there are Sang To (Double Butterfly sword) and medium-length pole (not long pole, but eyebrow height). These two weapons are nothing more than extensions of the hands.

Lin Xiang Fuk

If you only want to learn how to protect yourself when something happens, you really don't need to engage in free-fighting to achieve good self-defense skills.

Gorden Lu

We have training called dar wai, which is fighting in a circle, and other more advanced sparring training. This type of training allows students to become proficient in free fighting so they can handle street fights.

Alan Lee

Actually, chi sao serves many purposes. During the initial training period, chi sao provides a lot of different benefits. It develops a certain sensitivity and a certain kind of muscle tone.

Jim Lau

Wing Chun is a deadly art built to incapacitate an opponent in the shortest possible time. It's designed for a real situation, not for the ring or sport.

Gary Lam

There are actually several mainland versions of wing chun. Briefly, Joseph Cheng focused more on forty-five degree fighting stances and diagonal footwork. Also, he emphasized wing chun as more of a "hard" style.

Alan Lamb

If you put on gloves then it becomes a matter of winning points, which is not total fighting. Martial arts techniques can be adapted to be used with gloves but is not the same.

Wong Shun Leung

By studying other styles, you can really appreciate the simplicity and directness of the Wing Chun style. This is what I have been told by students who have studied other styles and have chosen to follow with Wing Chun path now.

Samuel Kwok

Bruce Lee was not only a talented actor, but also an outstanding martial artist. He developed his own martial arts philosophy, which he made known as "Jeet Kune Do", which emphasized the principles of efficiency, speed, and adaptability.

Mohammed Ince

"BlitzDefense" is only an exercise and wants to be no more and no less than an "applied, simplified Wing Tsun for the beginner" who seeks a fast route to self-defense.

Keith R. Kernspecht

Once the student has become proficient with "sern chi," he should next learn how to use sticking hands to both attack and defend against the partner. This is known as "qor sao" and it eventually develops into a full-blown fighting format.

Victor Kan

Chi Sao is like an application of techniques or movements that a student learns from the form. It should also be practiced daily.

Jim Fung

I don't think in terms of styles. If it's a "style," then there is a limitation. I think that it's important to focus on the individual and what he/she is capable of, and one's development. Everybody is comfortable to do what they love to do.

Francis Fong

In the Butterfly Knives, they are not necessarily eight directions in the movements. It refers to the lines the butter- fly knives describe in motion. The number eight looks like the two lines coming down to a point...similar to the chopping motion of the knives. It is about the mark that is made by the knives when you slash with them.

Augustine Fong

I believe Wing Chun is good for self-defense because it is direct and does not use fancy movements. It is meant to be used I close to the attacker.

Ip Chun

When I was young, I looked for training and techniques that could help me to fight better. Today, I am still looking for training and techniques that can help me to fight better.

Chung Kwok Chow

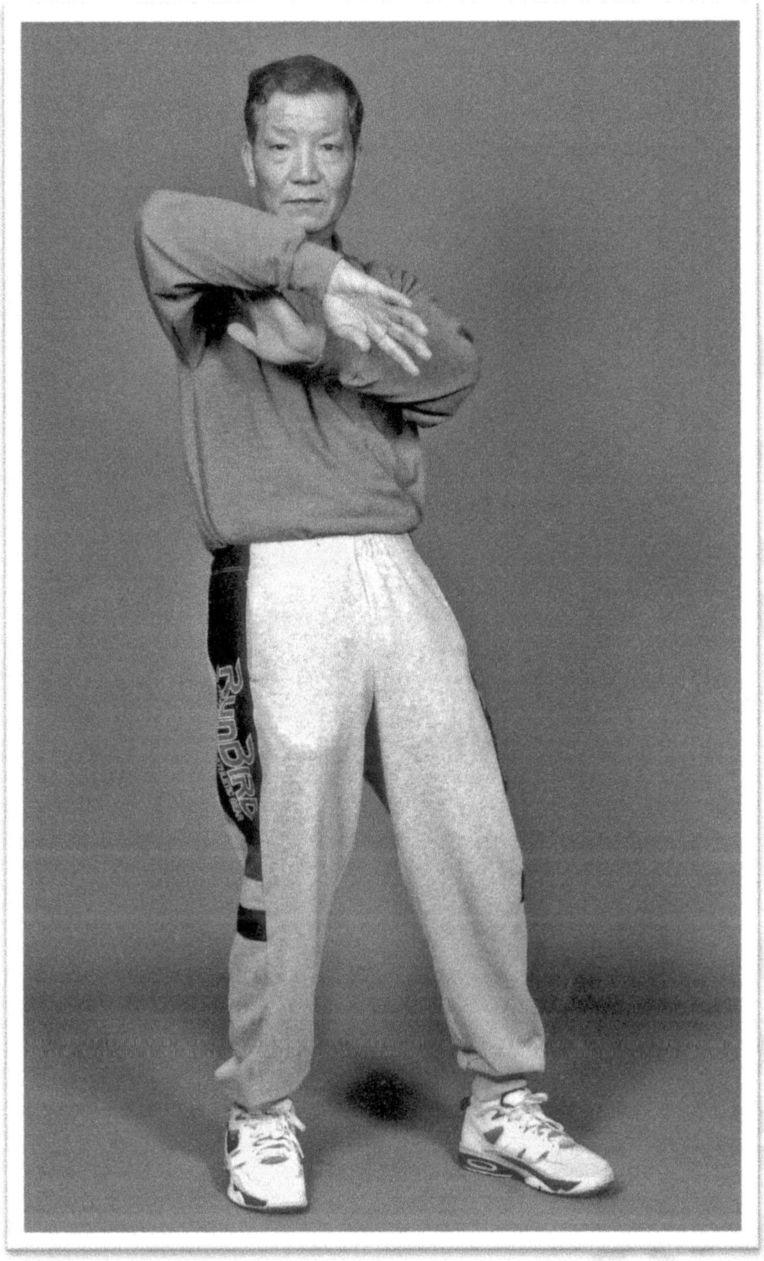

Keep your balance, break the opponent's and finish the fight without giving any chance to the aggressor.

Leung Ting

Chum Kiu uses this sequence, the tools and the lessons learnt from developing Siu Nim Tao and then builds on that, in a mobile, more complex, two-handed spatial awareness sequence of movements and combinations.

Shaun Rawcliffe

Wing Chun has two fighting styles—the short bridge and the long bridge.

Gorden Lu

The "Siu Nim Tau" and "Cham Kiu" forms encompass all the most essential skills and concepts of the Wing Chun system. They are the basis of everything that we do in combat.

David Peterson

I retired after a 25-plus-year career in public safety, where I worked as a police officer, firefighter, and emergency medic. I have been on the street. I know what a real fight is. The difference between sport and street application is as far away as east is from west.

Tony Massengill

In essence, the martial intent behind the weapons is lost. Weapons skills in the United Sates have degraded into a show; basically everyone wants to dazzle people—but it's empty.

Robert Chu

The student needs only to find a good teacher. Fortunately, there are competent teachers all over the world, but the student must be sure to find a good one, as there are a lot of bad ones as well!

Ip Ching

In Chum Kiu you start to move; you use the "big bow" (provide an illustration of this concept) and "bridge the gap" (provide an illustration of this concept) with the use of footwork and "seeking the bridge."

Samuel Kwok

Yip Man said to me that what he was going to teach me I shouldn't teach to anyone. That was his secret and his knowledge. The day he passed away that know ledge would be mine and only I had the right to teach it.

William Cheung

Chi Sao training is for you to get information on your opponent, but if you don't have the contact and are at a distance, you must rely on your eyes. Eye sensitivity takes over when you don't have the contact with your opponent; contact sensitivity takes over when you're jammed up and/or in close.

Hawkins Cheung

Chum Kiu is the second form, and it emphasizes the footwork and kicking techniques of the Wing Chun system; the basic ones of course.

Stephen Chan

When you have achieved a certain level in Wing Chun, you will need to concentrate on applications more, like Chi Sao training. Of course, that doesn't mean you don't need to train your forms anymore. I would say it depends on what level you are at.

Au Yeung

It doesn't really matter how good you are; it always boils down to the techniques. It's important to point out that I have never started a fight and I have never boasted about my victories.

Emin Boztepe

In modern times, Wing Chun should incorporate scientific self-defense methods while still upholding traditional martial arts values. A structured curriculum that efficiently delivers training and educates students on the system's effectiveness is essential.

William Kwok

By gaining and maintaining contact with an opponent's arm or arms, it is possible to control their movements, restrict their ability to use force and to close down their attacks, whilst allowing the Wing Chun practitioner to deploy a counterattack based upon the weaknesses felt or created through that contact.

Shaun Rawcliffe

"Chi Sau" provides a laboratory in which one can experiment on subtle skills and enhance reactions and reflexes that sparring or other combat-oriented drills cannot replicate.

David Peterson

Even though Hong Kong is a mecca of Kung Fu, I have not practiced any other Kung Fu style other than Wing Chun.

Donald Mak

Wing Chun emphasizes simplicity of use, economy of motion, and practicality. These three should guide a student's training. If what you are practicing does not meet these three criteria, the method needs to be reevaluated.

Tony Massengill

The second form, Cham Kiu, teaches you the functions of each action and how to utilize them in the right manner, such as hitting and defending against moving targets.

Gary Lam

Tao (known as "Siauw Lim Do" in HKB) is an introduction to the ABCs of the system. Chum Kiu (known as "Tim Kiao" in HKB) is to understand the wheel bearing body. Bil Jee (known as "Piao Ki" in HKB) is to acquire the skill of adapting and changing in a combat situation.

Lin Xiang Fuk

In Chum Kiu the student learns how to apply the tools developed in the first form against an opponent. In this form footwork is trained and the stu- dent encounters the principle of Yiu Ma - "Waist Energy". It is here that the student begins to learn the power base of Wing Chun.

Ip Ching

Beginners need to understand the ideas behind each move and do it right. When students start to learn chi- sao then they need to more focus on that, but they still doing the form everyday just to reinforce and refine the skills.

Gorden Lu

I would also advise a martial arts instructor to remain a good student for his entire life. If you are a meticulous note-taker and have a great memory, coupled with actually going home and diligently training what you have learned, seen and heard, it is possible to improve your skills even without constant supervision from an instructor.

Randy Williams

Fighting with martial arts skills is partly a branch of learning, and partly an art.

Wong Shun Leung

In my school, I teach students to apply Wing Chun techniques in practical situations. This requires that attackers go for real (though in the beginning, they can begin light and slow), because if you cannot handle it in the classroom, you cannot handle it in the street.

Alan Lee

Chum Kiu teaches you body unity. It shows how to use the hands and the body as a sole unit. The body is the foundation of the hand movement. With a strong body foundation all the hand techniques are much better and powerful.

Augustine Fong

In wing chun, there is a technical distinction between the fighting stance and the training stance. The training stance is governed by learning demands and tends to be more open to the opponent.

Jim Lau

The first form, Siu Lim Tao, I consider to be the "essential" form because without it basically you can't progress. It contains the basis and the fundamental techniques that you need to study Chi Sao and to get into the core of the system.

Leung Ting

The pole was not part of the original Wing Chun system, having been introduced by a Buddhist monk, Chi Tsin Sim See, some years after its founding by Ng Mei. Training in the long pole includes many aspects of Wing Chun theory including directness, focus and deflection.

Jim Fung

The weaponry forms are extensions of the empty hand forms, utilizing the same basic principles, movements, and muscles, so they are just as important as any other part of the system.

Samuel Kwok

I am not in favor of so-called dead, i.e. fixed or pre-arranged techniques. I have managed to get by with fewer than six moves (combinations). Any further movement would be one too many to learn.

Keith R. Kernspecht

Siu Nim Tao is an important form because it contains most of Ving Tsun's hand techniques. It also trains students in stance work and helps them develop their chi. Students should spend at least 15 minutes practicing Siu Nim Tao.

Victor Kan

Wing Chun should be used as a tool, not just a style. If you don't open your mind, you cannot learn. The most important thing is what you really want, and how you establish what you are looking for.

Francis Fong

The term "six and a half" in the Long Pole doesn't mean the amount of techniques, like many people think! It refers to the way you hit the target. If you bring the right force to the tip of the pole, the right vibration will cause the tip of the pole to leave a six and a half mark on the target.

Augustine Fong

The weapons introduce some footwork not found elsewhere in Wing Chun, which does help the empty hand method. So I believe the skills developed by weapons training is important to today's students.

Ip Chun

I was a natural with two skills necessary for kung fu—my observation skills, and my hand/leg coordination. I developed them early in my life by playing and learning in the streets, where everyone made a living by using their eyes and hands. It was also because I started to train in kung fu when I was a teenager.

Chung Kwok Chow

I used to think the skill in Hong Kong or China must be superior to the rest of the world, but after I visited in 1987 and later saw people who trained on the mainland, I was not impressed with the level of skill.

Robert Chu

Free-fighting or Chi Sao is necessary in order to develop an understanding of the proper timing, pressure, energy and application.

Ip Ching

Yip Man learned wing chun from two different masters. The first was Chan Wah Sun. This version was based on the centerline, and it is the wing chun version that you see in most schools today. But there's an older version of the art that is not based on the centerline, and this is the version the late Yip Man learned from Leung Bik, his second master.

William Cheung

If a Wing Chun practitioner can master superior timing, he can be free from the style. If you master timing, the style is secondary.

Hawkins Cheung

Bil Jee form only focus on attacking moves. There are eight attacking moves in Bil Jee: the elbow strikes, the Man Sao, the Bil Sao, Kan Sao, the Lap Sao and the Chop Kuen.

Stephen Chan

Wing Chun style concentrates on the centerline, close-range combat, and does not encourage meeting force with force. More importantly, it focuses on using hand and leg movements at the same time to maximize fighting efficiency.

Au Yeung

I did Turkish Wrestling before even I decided to start learning Wing Tsun and Escrima. I never underestimated a wrestler because I always knew what a good grappler can do to you once he passes the striking distance and takes you to the ground.

Emin Boztepe

I would recommend endurance training and strength training to Wing Tsun training. First, it is a good balance to martial arts training and second, it builds mindset and is good for the soul. You can improve your cardiovascular fitness through regular endurance training, be it running, cycling, swimming or other endurance sports. Good endurance will allow you to last longer during training and in fights and reduce fatigue.

Mohammed Ince

Chi Sao is a close quarter, contact oriented, continually moving training exercise, which enables the Wing Chun practitioner to develop the sensitivity and awareness to be able to feel and directly respond to an opponent's movement through contact.

Shaun Rawcliffe

The Hek Ki Boen Eng Chun System focuses on "detachment" as the main goal, through occupying the time, becoming the space, and explosive energy.

Lin Xiang Fuk

Like the forms, "Chi Sau" training imparts different levels of skill and allows for the development of both concepts and attributes that might otherwise go without improvement if not practiced in this way.

David Peterson

The pole also adds to the student's Wing Chun, but I believe to a much lesser degree. The pole is so different in structure from what we normally think of in empty hand Wing Chun that many people do not see the relationship.

Tony Massengill

Teaching beginning and intermediate level students will keep his basics sharp, but an instructor must also focus on his own personal maintenance and development of advanced techniques.

Randy Williams

A lot of moves and techniques may be easy to copy, but it is hard to be an expert. If you don't understand or if someone does not tell you correctly the lesson behind the technique or exercise, or you are not really focused on some details, then you will have huge gaps.

Gorden Lu

Students who learn the weapons properly gain increased understanding of the empty-hand techniques in a different or more skillful way.

Alan Lee

Siu Nim Tao and Chum Kiu are very closely intertwined, Chum Kiu being a logical extension of Siu Nim Tao training.

Shaun Rawcliffe

The art of wing chun, particularly through its three empty-hand and, one wooden dummy, and two weapons forms can represent an essentially complete overview of human kinesiology.

Jim Lau

Since I had a background in karate and Thai boxing, I was used to having my bodyweight on the front leg which messed up my WT footwork in the beginning. It felt awkward to me to rest my weight on the rear leg when I stepped, to squeeze my knees together in order to prevent kicks to the groin and to keep the upper body square as opposed to leaning into my punches.

Thommy L. Boehlig

A real fight on the street takes seconds, not minutes, and the aim of the game should be to end it as quickly as possible.

David Peterson

When choosing a martial arts school, we should prioritize finding a knowledgeable and skilled teacher for our training goals over a particular style. While the principles and techniques of a particular martial art can provide a framework for learning, it is up to the practitioner to apply them effectively.

William Kwok

Studying mainland style wing chun definitely helped me to make the form of wing chun that I now teach more complete.

Alan Lamb

Self-defense, health, and tradition all are important, but I'd say Wing Chun is more focused on self-defense.

Gary Lam

Wing Tsun training should be used to build your confidence in dealing with a physical altercation. It is this confidence that eventually will defeat the bullies.

Leung Ting

Fighting abilities are based on perseverance, confidence, and physical power-not talk.

Wong Shun Leung

Chi Sao is the closest exercise to fighting and it is important to Chi Sao, on a regular basis. And have your teacher advise you why you have left "openings" in your defense.

Samuel Kwok

In my book "Essence of Wing Tsun"—beyond techniques and thinking in applications" I assert that "Everything important is already taught in the first lesson."

Keith R. Kernspecht

The main characteristics of what became known as the Ving Tsun system are its economy of movement, directness of action, its vertical straight fist, its sticking hands and its use of the centerline theory.

Victor Kan

The Muk Yan Chong is a training tool that helps you correct angles and techniques while doing the form. As your training progresses you should be able to free flow on the dummy and not just stick to the form alone. There is no substitute for a real training partner.

Carson Lau

Chum Kiu utilizes the mobility taught by Sil Lum Tao by adding extra power. It teaches how to coordinate body and arm movements, utilizing multi-vectors of force to deflect and attack with maximum power.

Jim Fung

The third form, Biu Jee, focuses on speed, iron fingers for long-range strikes, and elbow strikes for close range strikes. Students learn to intercept the line, recover the line, and create the line.

Francis Fong

Gulao Wing Chun does not use the wooden dummy because its use will train you to keep at a distance from your opponent when the goal is to fight at a closer range.

Donald Mak

In the application of any method of Kung Fu in self-defense, you must get the idea of the limitations created by rules of a sport out of mind. There are no limited targets or methods of striking in a real self-defense situation.

Ip Chun

Chi Sao helps to develop the 13 principles of combat: posture, position, timing, distance, power, reaction, guts, the way, aggressiveness, control- ling, decision, reserve and adjustment.

Augustine Fong

The teacher can present the knowledge, but he cannot develop the skill for the student, that is up to the student.

Ip Ching

Hawkins taught me something great, he said, "Yip Man would tell us not to believe him regarding application of the art, but to test out our wing chun for ourselves." I think this statement had a profound effect on me.

Robert Chu

The most important point is sensitivity. Without sensitivity, you could have hundreds of techniques but not know how to use them. Sensitivity tells you when to use something (timing), how to use something (leverage), and what to use (technique).

Chung Kwok Chow

If you stop the punch at the elbow, the force is less, so it is easier. The elbow is easy to watch and block and will always indicate the movement of the punch.

William Cheung

In the world of Wing Chun, there are many different names, but they all share the same original principles and generally have the same three empty-hand forms as the building block.

William Kwok

Fighting is based on shocking attack. To shock the opponent with a blow or through surprise will slow or stop his attack.

Hawkins Cheung

The wooden dummy form has 8 sections. Within these 8 sections there are 8 kind of kicking techniques, the highest of the kicking techniques will not go up beyond the waist level. It is all groin kicks and knee kicks.

Stephen Chan

The essence of Ving Tsun is to use the simplest techniques to achieve goals in the shortest time and distance possible.

Kim Man Chan

I don't really think you need to go to free-fight tournament in order to be a good fighter. Of course, if you do this will benefit your skill and experience but we need to differentiate between a free-fight championship and a real fight.

Emin Boztepe

I want to get my students/instructors to the highest standard possible, so I have some excellent hands to train and practice with between my trips to Hong Kong.

Shaun Rawcliffe

We are not in the business of self-defense—it is an unrealistic expectation to think that one can merely defend oneself—we are in the business of learning to fight better than our opponent.

David Peterson

The knives add a lot to the student's empty hand skills. There are footwork and angles that do not exist elsewhere in the system. So, I would say that the knives are a very important aspect of Wing Chun training.

Tony Massengill

When you see an effective technique, you can't be afraid to work back-wards and to break it down and see why it works-then try to use movements from your own style to create a similar application.

Randy Williams

Actually, in our family system, these three forms are not necessarily the core forms. We have several others.

Lin Xiang Fuk

Everybody who learns Wing Chun should know chi-sao is the heart of the art and the first form is the most important form of the system.

Gorden Lu

Although technique training and circle fighting are useful to learn the application of Wing Chun, this is still not fighting.

Alan Lee

Each individual merely expresses to the best of their ability their own understanding of a style. It is somehow inappropriate to make public comparisons since they are of such a purely personal nature.

Jim Lau

Biu Jee opens our eyes to emergency and abnormal situations. Each form is very useful and interrelated.

Gary Lam

The Muk Yan Chong form teaches us a different set of maneuvers that are extremely effective in combat. There are a series of principles that are intrinsic only to the wooden dummy training and can be used in both Chi Sao and self-defense.

Leung Ting

Chi Sao training helps the person to react without thinking. Due to the sensitivity training, the person learns to redirect any energy that is oncoming and use the Fan Sao technique in conjunction with the footwork of the style.

Samuel Kwok

Wanting to avoid mistakes like good Confucians, it starts with the smallest details and the extremities that are furthest away from the central axis. With the 2nd form (Cham Kiu) it gets closer and closer to the central axis as the source of power and moves on to the 3rd form.

Keith R. Kernspecht

Wing Chun curriculum differ depending what lineage you belong to. The Leung Ting method (Leung Ting is my si-gung, my "sifu's sifu") is known for its extensive and well-thought through Chi Sao sections (two men forms that consist of Chi Sao drills).

Thommy L. Boehlig

Unlike many other styles, Ving Tsun does not oppose the opponent's force with force because in that case the stronger person will nearly always win.

Victor Kan

Bil Tse adds extra power through physical acceleration of the body. For example, when pivoting in Wing Chun, the top and bottom sections of the body move together. Bil Tse trains the student how to move the top sec- tion of the body further, giving greater and faster reach in striking.

Jim Fung

In today's world, personal safety is of utmost importance. More and more people are looking for ways to protect themselves and gain a sense of security. In light of this growing demand, I would like to focus more on self-defense. I am committed to reaching as many people as possible and teaching them the skills of self-defense.

Mohammed Ince

The Muk Jong or wooden dummy is used to find the correct line in the execution of the movement and incorporates techniques from the three empty hand forms. It teaches you the principle of the centerline, triangle, gates, timing, etc.

Augustine Fong

"Chum Kiu" begins teaching the coordination of the hands learned in the Siu Lim Tao, with the horse stance and stepping introduced at this phase of training. Chum Kiu teaches directional changes along with shifting and stepping. Also, this form introduces kicking.

Ip Chun

Physically, one has less time to train when he gets older, so one has to continue to practice basic "gung" (work)—that is, basic exercises to maintain strength, flexibility, and timing. Nothing leaves the basics. Advanced work is just the basics applied.

Robert Chu

My reputation as street fighter became very big and my family was not happy with that. I didn't feel very comfortable being at home—I couldn't find much warmth in the house.

William Cheung

The forms give the student the proper structure for the techniques employed in Chi Sao. Chi Sao teaches the student application, use of energy, direction of energy and sensitivity. Chi Sao teaches the student how to control the opponent.

Ip Ching

In Ip Man Wing Chun, we focus on the first gate (wrist) and second gate (forearm), whereas Gulao Wing Chun stresses the third gate (rear arm and shoulder), which is a more "sticky body" range.

Donald Mak

Believing that one has mastered a technique would cause the person to stop practicing, and their training will decline.

William Kwok

Siu Lim Tao is the most important form of the whole system. The form doesn't just teach the hand movements and structures. The most important is to let practitioners know the idea behind each move.

Gorden Lu

All the above forms are different expressions of the basic ideas of Wing Chun, although each form has a different emphasis.

Alan Lee

Wing Chun is a very sophisticated system of self-defense. It originated from Shaolin master Ng Mui. Ng Mui combined the best from Shaolin with her own experiences and understanding to create the style of Wing Chun.

Augustine Fong

When you do chi sao, you should not attack first, but rather try to collect as much information as you can on your opponent. Many Wing Chun practitioners want to attack first without gathering information. Attacking first is to give your opponent information on yourself.

Hawkins Cheung

My Wing Chun system has only one goal; to destroy the opponent. A lot of people think that if you are good in Chi Sao or sticking hands, you are a automatically a "fighter."

Stephen Chan

I don't do much weight training. But I recommend have a good cardiovascular program and any kind of isometric power training with your own body since this is great for your tendons and ligaments.

Emin Boztepe

I believe if you teach the forms, drills and Chi Sao correctly, honestly and openly on a technical level, then those seeking self-defense will find that and be able to use and steer their Wing Chun in that way.

Shaun Rawcliffe

You cannot train for sport and have the "combat fairy" tap you on the head with his magic wand and make you react properly for the "real world."

Tony Massengill

"Learning how to teach" is very important. I also will emphasize to my students if they want to teach Wing Chun one day, because we are not just teaching people Wing Chun but also increasing the students' understanding of the art, helping them to develop their Wing Chun style, and letting them acquire this life skill.

Gorden Lu

Wing Chun, unlike some other styles, is designed for fighting only. The most important principle in Wing Chun is simultaneous offense and defense; that is, defense is offense and offense is defense.

Alan Lee

The wing chun system has a very precise method for preparing a student for combat. This training method includes three empty-hand forms, a set of 108 wooden dummy techniques, Muk Yan Jong, a long pole form, Luk Dim Bun Gwun, and a short knives form, Bot Jeom Do.

Jim Lau

In Wing Chun, we do not block the attack, we deflect it and simultaneously attack in one motion; we do not chase the limbs, but always attack the center of mass.

David Peterson

Siu Nin Tao covers the basics and foundation of Wing Chun, like the alphabet: A, B, C, D.

Gary Lam

The concepts and principles behind Siu Nim Tao, Chum Kiu, and Biu Jee forms are absolutely essential and interconnected to each other.

Kim Man Chan

We do have a series of cycles in Chi Sao but these cycles are only a way of organizing the material so that the student knows exactly where it comes from and how these techniques belong to certain empty hand forms.

Leung Ting

A Wing Chun practitioner should never lose the "initial contact" with the opponent. In addition, the Bil Jee form teaches you to improve your speed for attacking (feeling when there is an opening in your opponent's defense

Samuel Kwok

In the end the Wing Tsun master as I imagine him should not be distinguishable by specific movements, but by a way of moving that is "unspecific"—a term I did not invent but which I consider to be apt.

Keith R. Kernspecht

Bruce Lee was an intelligent and ambitious young man who realized that the only way that others would acknowledge his own talents and achievements was to break away from tradition and establish himself as a figurehead of his own right.

Victor Kan

Siu Lim Tao, the student, is given the introduction to the defensive and offensive tools as well as the root stance from which the fighting footwork will be based.

Ip Ching

The "short bridge" method is close range fighting, tight and nail on the opponent, and emphasizes quick response and continuous follow-up with various combinations of control techniques, strikes, and kicks.

Gorden Lu

When describing the structure of the Wing Tsjun system (Wing Tsjun being the branding my school uses to highlight the curriculum that specifies what we teach within my organization), I like to use the model of a circle that consists of a number of "pizza slices" as they relate to how they deal with an opponent's force.

Thommy L. Boehlig

The "Biu Jee" form teaches about recovery from mistakes made in a fight, and also how to deal with angles that have not been covered in the first two forms. Relaxation is emphasized in this form to produce a soft energy. Trained together, these forms help the student develop into a more safe and secure individual.

Ip Chun

The butterfly knives are used as an extension of the arm, and some movements are very similar to empty hand movements like bong dau or bong sau. Chung do (piercing) is similar to punching.

Jim Fung

Biu Jee is the last empty hand form. One of the myths is that "Biu Jee does not go out the door." This doesn't mean that it is a secret form or anything.

Augustine Fong

Siu Lim Tao means "a little idea." The primary purpose of the first form is to focus on fundamentals—basic structure, energy, position, and understanding of the centerline theory. Controlling the *Dan Tin* trains the chi.

Francis Fong

Some people mentioned to me that my Muk Jong form is different than others wooden dummy forms. I can't say anything else but that I teach the same form taught to me by my Sifu Ho Kam Ming.

Augustine Fong

The truth is one either develops body structure or doesn't. With advanced practitioners of wing chun—the lineage isn't important—what I noticed was only a small handful of people had body structure. Most didn't.

Robert Chu

Trapping is the heart of Wing Chun. Sun Tzu wrote that all warfare is based upon deception, and to trap an opponent is to deceive him. When I trap your hand, your leg, or your body, your mind instantly freezes and considers the options.

Hawkins Cheung

Reflective teaching involves critically examining my instructive approaches and adjusting my methods based on their effectiveness. Conversely, reflective learning enables me to analyze past experiences to identify successful and unsuccessful aspects of my practice.

William Kwok

Only a responsible teacher will press for the perfection of techniques; the quality of the student is what counts, not quantity.

Victor Kan

Wing Chun is built on a foundation of simplicity and efficiency. Kicks are to low targets, application is at close range, which is where real fights occur. Reflex action is built by way of sensitivity training drills, which make the application of defense and attack much more reliable.

Ip Ching

I train Wing Chun seven days a week with the help of weight training. I do emphasize the weight training because I actually have practiced weight training since I was about 18 years old.

Stephen Chan

Chi Sao is a unique training method, which develops sensitivity and contact reflexes in the arms, allowing the practitioner to assess the situation and to perceive and deflect the opponent's force as soon as they come into contact with their opponent's arms.

Shaun Rawcliffe

If you only ever train against a fellow Wing Chun exponent, and not "pressure-test" your Wing Chun, your "Chi Sau" skills alone are just not enough.

David Peterson

The "long bridge" is more distance-fighting—move in fast and get out fast. It emphasizes good body structure with crash in power and flexibility to provide different combination strikes and kicks.

Gorden Lu

Concentrate on proper structure in technique. Practice dynamic footwork. Make sure that your footwork is supporting your hand.

Tony Massengill

Your expression of the style will be somehow different than your teacher or fellow students regardless of how closely you follow the traditional patterns.

Randy Williams

The "Muk Yan Jong" (wooden dummy) form then provides us with ways of recovering from the kinds of typical errors that can occur in combat, as well as enhancing our ability to utilize the best distancing, timing and angles.

David Peterson

Wing Chun is very abstract. Wing Chun is art. Wing Chun is like painting, you can use different colors in the painting, or you can just use one color to make the same painting.

Gorden Lu

Many just do forms, sticky hands, and believe they have completed the Wing Chun curriculum. This is laughable because the forms and sticky hands are only the beginning of the whole syllabus.

Alan Lee

Bruce Lee had the integrity to call what he taught by another name, rather than mislead people. If someone is claiming to teach "Ip Man Wing Chun," the system they teach should be recognizable as what Ip Man taught.

Samuel Kwok

A wing chun practitioner must preserve and protect his own centerline while, at the same time, breaking and invading the opponent's centerline. This maxim of combat is accomplished by constantly pushing forward, controlling the opponent's arms, and narrowing the distance between you and him.

Jim Lau

Wing Tsun begins with the "Siu Nim Tau" form, though its primary purpose may not be learning mere techniques, but rather mental training or unifying oneself. Training our attentiveness and power of imagination, while in an apparently motionless stance.

Keith R. Kernspecht

In the Siu Nim Tau form, we learn hand techniques from a standing and stationary position. Our hands move right, left and center without moving our bodies. In Gulao Wing Chun, when performing similar techniques, you can pivot your body to let your hand be placed on the right, left or center without moving your hand.

Donald Mak

My master once likened the three forms to the components of a motor vehicle, with Sil Lum Tao as the chassis or framework, Chum Kiu the engine, and Bil Tse, the turbocharger.

Jim Fung

The important points to teaching Wing Chun is to get the student to trust the structure of the technique, and not depend too much on muscular strength to overcome the opponent.

Ip Chun

Biu jee is based on the first two forms, Siu Lim Tao and Chum Kiu and if you don't know Biu Jee you can't really know and understand the second part of the wooden dummy form. This one of the reasons why there are so many different wooden dummy forms around!

Augustine Fong

Siu Nim Tao is a static, solo, simple, single handed (when both hands are utilized, the left mirrors the right.

Shaun Rawcliffe

The art of Wing Chun is flexible in that it allows for personal expression. Personal expression is the art part.

Robert Chu

The pole training develops the students' power and understanding. The knives have footwork and principles not found in the empty hand system. These things will enhance the students empty hand skills.

Ip Ching

While the "Biu Ji" form shows us ways of escaping relatively unharmed should all of the essential elements fail due to outstanding circumstances, such as being caught completely by surprise.

David Peterson

Bil Jee is the last form and most dynamic by focusing on short-range power and sudden changes in distance, both vertically and horizontally. It uses techniques to close the gap or create distance depending on the situation.

William Kwok

It was interesting to me was to experience what real fights feel like and how differently the brain reacts to the stress they create. Sometimes a fight seemed to happen in a split second, your body just functions and you can't really get a grip with what just happened until the situation is over.

Thommy L. Boehlig

You have basically two methods of capturing the centerline: the first is to have superior speed over the opponent, and the second is to start entering just as the opponent attacks. The key and determining factor is timing.

Hawkins Cheung

In 1978, I went back to Hong Kong to further my studies of Wing Chun. I was blessed with the opportunity to study with the two sons of Great Grandmaster Ip Man, Grandmasters Ip Chun and Ip Ching.

Samuel Kwok

It was believed that weight training slows you down, but I proved differently, and I encourage students to train with weights along with Wing Chun training. You must train alongside it. You just can't do weights and then stop Wing Chun training because it has to go together.

Stephen Chan

The simple reason being that Wing Chun is a systematic set of tools that you must learn to apply appropriately and accordingly yourself. To quote Sifu, "Wing Chun doesn't define you—you define your Wing Chun."

Shaun Rawcliffe

As such, styles often only suit certain individuals who have certain athletic talents, but do not provide the "common man" with methods that can easily be applied.

David Peterson

Training at the time was very hard. The teachers were very traditional, and you have to prove your dedication and loyalty, or you were going to learn nothing at all. They demanded a lot from the students but once you got to actually learn, the experience was incomparable.

Augustine Fong

I have had the opportunity to train in both Hong Kong and Foshan, China. I found that like America, some practitioners are good, and some not so good. A lot depends on the focus of the instructor.

Tony Massengill

Chi-sao is the heart of Wing Chun and Ip Man used to say, "the older you are the better you will get on Chi-sao"—which means your Wing Chun study should never finish.

Gorden Lu

I still do a siu leem tau or chum kiu, a 45-minute footwork pattern, and a thousand kicks and punches at least once a week to this day.

Randy Williams

Chum Kiu form is important in that it focuses on the turning and using Yu Ma— turning the legs and hips to generate the energy (as a whirlpool of the spinning top)—to redirect energy away from your centerline.

Samuel Kwok

Traditionally that is probably true. But as my Wing Tsun Sifu Leung Ting once wrote, tradition means "Nothing has been improved!"

Keith R. Kernspecht

There are two main points in my teaching methods. First, I emphasize the practical application of the style, and for this there are a lot of different kinds of training. The second main point of my teaching method is that students must analyze for themselves how and why things work or do not work.

Alan Lee

All the Wing Tsun forms are extremely important because they teach certain principles that are unique to each one of them.

Leung Ting

In theory, wing chun stresses simplicity, directness, economy, and completeness. Simplicity means that movements and techniques should be clean and uncomplicated. Directness implies immediate effectiveness. Economy is the conservation of energy and effort.

Jim Lau

Engaging in free sparring is important as it helps build self-confidence.

Gary Lam

Chum Kiu emphasizes footwork, kicks, mobility, and hand leg coordination and also expands the ideas of using the movements from the first form to be a technique or a way of application in a close-range fighting.

Gorden Lu

The Wing Chun style of Kung Fu is very good for practical self-defense. Some styles have too many forms and too many movements in each form—they are too complicated. This is not the case with the Ip Man Family Wing Chun Kung Fu style.

Samuel Kwok

Chum Kiu introduces more complex footwork. It emphasizes controlling the distance between the practitioner and the opponent, using longer-range techniques and footwork.

William Kwok

Any style of kung fu needs good foundation work without which the students will be unable to reach the higher levels of training. The speed of progress actually rests on how much the students are willing to put themselves into the training.

Victor Kan

Sil Lum Tao is the most important because it forms the foundation of the whole Wing Chun system. Unless you are very good at Sil Lum Tao, you are wasting your time trying to learn the other forms.

Jim Fung

The primary purpose of the second form, Chum Kiu, is understanding movement. Chum Kiu trains the stance and the waist, using footwork and rotation. The entire body moves as one unit.

Francis Fong

The meaning of Biu Jee is not to use fingers to poke the opponent's eyes, but to employ shooting or thrusting techniques in emergency situations, to deflect and penetrate an attack.

Augustine Fong

"Siu Lim Tao" is the starting gate for all Wing Chun skill. It teaches the relaxation of the body and the best physical structure of the defensive and attacking movements of the system. In Siu Lim Tao the student is also introduced to elbow energy. This teaches how Wing Chun generates power in movement.

Ip Chun

In wing chun, nobody teaches you step by step what to do in "chi sao" (sticking hands) or what to do when attacked spontaneously—you have to develop yourself to utilize it.

Robert Chu

The teacher has to make sure all of the key points are understood, and the student has gained the necessary mastery of the foundation methods upon which more advanced methods are built.

Ip Ching

In other styles, movement originates from outside toward the center. Other styles choose to use the curved line. Wing Chun is different in that movement originates from the center outward. Wing Chun is designed to cut the motions from other systems.

Hawkins Cheung

I find it hard to define what 'Pure' Wing Chun is. Wing Chun has so many flavors. The keys I believe are to maintain the core concepts of Wing Chun through the forms, the interpretation and applications will always be and should be unique to the individual.

Shaun Rawcliffe

The "Luk Dim Boon Gwan" ("six-and-a-half-point pole") is an excellent way to develop and enhance the Wing Chun student's wrist, waist and stance strength.

David Peterson

The Wing Chun long pole is longer than most other Chinese Kung Fu styles' pole or stick, so the Wing Chun pole is also heavier.

Gorden Lu

Ground and pound, for example, is a bad strategy when the ground is covered with broken glass and gravel or has bottles and rocks that can be grabbed by the opponent and used as a weapon against you. Third parties often enter street fights. When you are on the ground, you can only deal with one opponent.

Tony Massengill

Most Wing Chun movements have come easily to me. Of course, I still have had to practice extremely hard so I can make each movement completely natural and respond to an opponent's attack by reflex and instinct.

Alan Lee

Wing chun is essentially an art of maneuvers, specifically those designed to deal with practical fighting situations. Hence, formal bowing, artistic forms of dancing, symbolic imitations of animals and showy movements of any kind are not a part of this art.

Jim Lau

I haven't "mastered" the system, and I truly never will—I don't think anyone ever does!

David Peterson

At the end of the day the student finds the master according to what he is looking for in a style and the best we as teachers can do, is make sure that we work on our syllabus, teaching methodology and leadership abilities daily, to provide the best support possible for the student.

Thommy L. Boehlig

Siu Lim Tao focuses on structure and alignment, simplicity and efficiency, and keeping opponents close. The form emphasizes maintaining a strong stance and generating power from the body structure.

William Kwok

Grandmaster Yip Man knew that what he was teaching at that stage was slightly different in application from what he taught in his early days. I don't think he tried to teach something totally different, but his perception of the art was different because of his age.

Leung Ting

Everyone who learns and then passes a system on to a new generation of students brings some personal flavor to the system.

Ip Chun

For me, the Wing Chun style is very different from other styles, as it is based upon the "centerline" theory (the shortest distance between two points is a straight line). Wing Chun does not incorporate any 'flowery' techniques.

Samuel Kwok

Styles that look at function. Where function comes first, and then the form. Form follows function! Unfortunately, most styles start everything with the form.

Keith R. Kernspecht

Although I was the one who actually started Bruce in his first form training, I did not train with him much because his attendances were very irregular.

Victor Kan

In my experience weapons training enhances the student's empty-handed ability.

Thommy L. Boehlig

Sil Lum Tao is the most important because it forms the foundation of the whole Wing Chun system. Unless you are very good at Sil Lum Tao, you are wasting your time trying to learn the other forms.

Jim Fung

I haven't studied the Yip Man branch of Wing Chun, but I believe that there would be a lot of similarities in the systems, especially with the concepts and principles. It depends on the individual instructor.

Francis Fong

The forms develop important fundamentals and principles and like a time capsule, they preserve the knowledge and technique of the system. The three hand forms can be practiced individually or as one continuous form. Each form represents a different level of training.

Augustine Fong

When I went to Hawkins Cheung, I already knew the entire system and had practiced wing chun for over 11 years. Hawkins told me that knowing forms wasn't enough—I had to concentrate on application.

Robert Chu

Every student will perform differently based on a number of factors, such as body type, height, weight, past experience, and reason for learning.

Ip Ching

Wing Chun is designed as a combat system. For this reason, the system emphasizes confidence, timing, intercepting, capturing the centerline, shocking the opponent, setting up for consecutive strikes, and trapping.

Hawkins Cheung

For anyone to become proficient in Wing Chun, they must understand how their body works and how it can be used most efficiently and effectively. Wing Chun is a very scientific art based upon human anatomy.

Shaun Rawcliffe

The first form builds the foundation for the second. The second is pretty much the way we want to apply our techniques under ideal conditions. And the third is to save our backside when things don't go according to plan – which, by the way is almost always the case.

Tony Massengill

A lot of time when the person has not enough knowledge of that style he is teaching, he usually will create his own approach and that may not match original principles or will mislead the students to the wrong training.

Gorden Lu

The movements in the three forms contain some of Wing Chun's basic elements and ideas. In the beginning, because Wing Chun uses power in a scientific way.

Alan Lee

The real trademark and focus of wing chun training centers on sticking-hands practice, Chi Sao, which is exclusive to this art.

Jim Lau

Wing Tsun differs from other "Wing Chun" or "Ving Tsun" methods in that the main idea is not to memorize methods of reacting to any kind of attack.

Leung Ting

Something interesting happens when we teach: our brain finds new ways to describe a technique and by using our own words to describe them rather than our teacher's words, we achieve a deeper sense of certainty for said technique.

Thommy L. Boehlig

The most important thing in both teaching and learning Wing Chun, in order for the student to become proficient, is the correct development of the foundations of the system.

David Peterson

Actually, I am not very good at memorizing lots of movements and many forms. That's why I found Wing Chun a better style of kung fu for me to learn, but it takes many years to master.

Samuel Kwok

Leaving the 3rd form and perhaps the Wooden Dummy form aside, I think there is not enough flow when practicing the Wing Tsun/Wing Chun forms.

Keith R. Kernspecht

I personally do not train with weights but some of my students do. I believe that such a method of bodybuilding can complement the Ving Tsun system.

Victor Kan

Sil Lum Tao in its advanced stages helps the practitioner develop thought force (nim lik), which gives you enormous power and strengthens your whole body structure.

Jim Fung

The three forms of Wing Chun have a very specific purpose in the martial art education of the student. Practicing a form might involve training a hundred things at once, both internal and external.

Augustine Fong

In applying Wing Chun, you have to change to keep up with your opponent's change; your target is always moving. Wing Chun is a system that has no particular style.

Hawkins Cheung

I was no natural—in fact, I was rather skinny and uncoordinated when young. I was tall and lanky compared to the average Cantonese. I did have one advantage -- I had great flexibility with my legs, and usually beat most Southern fist practitioners with my legs.

Robert Chu

One of the main keys to learning Wing Chun is learning not to rely on muscular strength in the application of technique. One must learn to use the body as a whole to provide the needed power for the method.

Ip Ching

In Wing Chun, we always attempt to attack an attack with aggressive, scientifically-based methods of counter-fighting—we do not fight defensively at any stage if it can be avoided.

David Peterson

Check out these Other Great Titles from EMPIRE BOOKS!

VISIT **MartialArtsDigital.com**

WING CHUN MASTERS
By José M. Fraguas

#320 — 7" x 10" — approx. 380 pages
ISBN 13: 978-1-933901-52-7

Through conversations with many historical Wing Chun figures such as the Grandmaster Yip Man's sons; Yip Ching and Yip Chun, and other top disciples of his like Wong Shun Leung, Willian Cheung, Victor Kan, Leung Ting, and more, the information in this book has never appeared anywhere before. The author, José M. Fraguas proudly presents **Wing Chun Masters**, with an amazing repertoire of great masters and teachers of the art of Wing Chun Kung Fu.

In this volume, interviews with the world's top masters, like the "Kaiser of Wing Tsun," Keith R. Kernspecht, and other leading world instructors like Augustine Fong, Samuel Kwok, Francis Fong, Jim Lau, Gary Lam, Stephen Chan, and many more have been gathered to present an integrated and complete view of the "Beautiful Springtime" Chinese art of fighting, philosophy, and self-defense.

The late Master Jim Fung and outstanding world teachers like David Peterson, Robert Chu, Tony Massengill, Leo Au Yeung, Randy Williams, Chow K. Chung, Gorden Lu, and legendary fighter Emin Boztepe, amongst others, explain the many concepts and principles of the art in a clear manner that everyone can understand. Packed with dynamic photographs, this book presents the ins and outs of the philosophy of the art of Wing Chun.

This volume contains intriguing thoughts, fascinating personal details, hidden histories, and inspiring philosophies, as each master reveals his true love for the art and a deep understanding of every facet associated with the practice and spirit of the Chinese art of Wing Chun Kung Fu as a way of life. This invaluable reference book is a must-have addition to your personal library.

These and Other Outstanding Book and Video Titles In-Stock and Available NOW!

WING CHUN: TRADITIONAL WOODEN DUMMY
By Samuel Kwok & Tony Massengill

#318 — 7" x 10"
approx. 208 pages
ISBN 13: 978-1-933901-46-6

The Wing Chun wooden training dummy is a training device designed to correct technique and structure, as well as increase power, speed, accuracy, and conditioning.

Learn the true Original Ip Man's Wing Chun Wooden Dummy form from Grandmaster Samuel Kwok. This book is a complete, step-by-step guide to the Wooden Dummy hands techniques, legs application, and footwork. All the original sections are demonstrated clearly from start to finish, in different camera angles to facilitate easy and accurate learning. There also is a description of each segment and its most common training mistakes to improve not only your technique, but your level of understanding. In addition to teaching the skills on the wooden dummy, Grandmaster Samuel Kwok demonstrates the applications of the wooden dummy training techniques on a partner, giving an excellent idea of the combat effectiveness of each movement.

Order Online Now!

www.MartialArtsDigital.com

Many More Titles Available Online Now from EMPIRE BOOKS!

VISIT: MartialArtsDigital.com

MASTERING WING CHUN KUNG FU
By Samuel Kwok and Tony Massengill

In this book, the keys to the Ip Man Wing Chun Kung Fu system are explained. The three hand sets are shown in detail, along with the application of the key movements. One of the keys to Wing Chun is laying a proper foundation. The first form Siu Lim Tao (Little Idea) is the development of that foundation. While the first form teaches the correct structure of the attacks and defensive movements, it is in Chum Kiu that the student learns to "seek the bridge" and use both hands simultaneously, such as one hand defending while the other attacks. The third form, Biu Gee (Thrusting Fingers), also known as the (First Aid) form, teaches the keys to recovery from the loss of a superior position in fighting. Biu Gee training is one of the keys to learning to focus energy into a strike. Also covered is the Chi Sao (Sticking Hands) training of Wing Chun, as well as the key principles that have made Ip Man Wing Chun one of the most famous Kung Fu systems in the world.

#313 — 7" x 10" — approx. 304 pages
ISBN 13: 978-1-933901-26-8

Order Online Now!

www.MartialArtsDigital.com

www.ingramcontent.com/pod-product-compliance
Lightning Source LLC
Chambersburg PA
CBHW042359070526
44586CB00027B/2819